GROOMING DOGS
FOR PROFIT

Grooming Dogs for Profit

by Charlotte Gold

Photographs by
Michael G. Gold

FIRST EDITION

First Printing—1986

HOWELL BOOK HOUSE Inc.
230 Park Avenue
New York, N.Y. 10169

Library of Congress Cataloging-in-Publication Data

Gold, Charlotte, 1941-
  Grooming dogs for profit.

  1. Dog grooming industry.   I. Title.
SF427.55.G65   1986   636.7'08'33   86-14773
ISBN 0-87605-618-4

Printed in U.S.A.

To
Mother and Evelyn, who always knew I could;
Mariann and "Ande," for being special;
Bonnie and Nancy, who lived every chapter;
Dan Schroeder and Kenny Freeman, who knew me when;
All my canine clients and their owners;
But especially to:
My daughter Nikki for being the best there is
and
My husband Mike for loving me and being RIGHT!

Contents

Introduction

IF YOU PICKED this book up thinking to learn *how* to groom dogs, then you have chosen the wrong book entirely. There are many excellent books on grooming; this book deals with the business aspects of grooming for profit, rather than instruction on grooming. The entire book is directed to the person who is already well versed in grooming (whether of one breed or of many breeds) and who has been giving some thought to the idea of grooming for others and being paid for that service. While some ideas are presented for the individual interested in employment in the field of dog grooming, the majority of this work is aimed at the individual who is interested in opening a profitable business.

For those who believe that a dog grooming business would be an ideal occupation, but don't know too much about business or perhaps anything about grooming itself, it would be a good idea to try an apprenticeship program to learn the art and to try out the work itself. Then read this book so that you will have a firm grasp of the business aspect of the grooming salon. With practical experience and sound information about the mechanics of running a shop, you will be well equipped to make your own career decision.

If you have been involved with dogs for any length of time, whether as an exhibitor of show dogs, a breeder, or simply a well-informed owner, it has surely occurred to you that there is money to be made in offering services to pet owners. Witness the many businesses that revolve around these services: pet food companies, boarding kennels, pet equipment, toys and clothing, shampoos and home remedies, obedience training classes, pet cemeteries and many other more exotic services. And of course, there is pet grooming. These pet-oriented services add up to an enormous industry. In fact, analysis shows that far more money is to be made through services for pets than through the sale of pets.

As an example, imagine that a buyer spends $150 to purchase a pet Miniature Poodle puppy. If this hypothetical pup lives only ten years (not a really advanced age) his owner will easily spend a sum much greater than his purchase price for services. To break down costs let's look at this example: food will cost at least $5 per month, which totals a minimum of $720 over the projected ten-year life expectancy of this dog (more if the owner chooses to feed expensive canned or soft moist products); veterinary care for the normal healthy dog will average about $50 per year at today's prices, or $500 during our example dog's life (this does not make any allowance for serious illness or for almost inevitable inflation); collars, leashes, food dishes, toys and perhaps a dog-training class will certainly total at least $100 over a ten-year period; sending the little furry friend to a boarding kennel during family vacations could easily add up to $500; then there is grooming, our major concern—this dog could make nine, ten, or even twelve visits to the grooming shop each year—for a medium-size Poodle a yearly grooming bill might average $150 at a modestly priced shop, or a whopping $1,500 during that ten-year life span. Have you been keeping track? To make it easy for you, the total services for that imaginary pup over a ten-year period come to approximately $3,320. There is no exaggeration involved here at all—in fact, this is a very conservative estimate.

Can you see why the profit in dogs is to be found in services, not in the sale of animals? Did you notice that it was the grooming shop that had the largest share of the money spent on that dog? To be sure, there are lots of dogs who never see the inside of a grooming salon, but it certainly isn't just Poodles who make regular visits to the hairdresser. Spaniels of all kinds, terriers and Poodles are the most evident in the average shop; however, there are numerous coated breeds who require regular professional grooming, as well as the short-coated breeds who will be in for bathing, dips, and toenail trims. And don't forget the all-American mutt. Most groomers have quite a respectable representation of the K-9-X among their clientele, and the owners of these "guess-whats" take just as much pride in the appearance of their pets as do the owners of the pedigreed dogs.

It doesn't take a mathematical whiz to figure out that a grooming business can be a profitable venture. Since you are already an accomplished groomer (or are at least in the process of learning) let's examine this idea of grooming dogs for profit.

1

Ready for the Big Plunge . . .

Where Will You Work?

So. YOU ARE a groomer. You have decided you want to take up the grooming of dogs as a profession. Great! Now what? Do you have any options? Sure you do. You have quite a number of options, as a matter of fact. All of the options, as in any other field of endeavor, will require some thought and decision making on your part. The first decision you will need to make is whether you wish to work for someone else or open your own place of business.

If you choose to begin your career by working for someone else, there are several places that offer opportunities for a well-trained groomer.

THE ESTABLISHED SHOP

The first and most obvious option for a dog groomer is to seek employment in an established grooming shop. In a shop or salon you can generally expect to earn a percentage on each dog you groom. Sometimes it is possible to arrange a guaranteed minimum or a salary plus commission. This will vary with the custom that prevails in your particular part of the country, with the individual salon and with the degree of expertise you offer.

Some of the advantages of starting in this situation are plain: the shop is already in operation, you will have a ready-made clientele, a location with which the customers are familiar, a telephone listing and you will have appointments made for you. If the shop is a very busy one, it may also employ a bather who will take care of all bathing, and possibly drying, thus leaving you free to do the actual grooming and enabling you to do more dogs per day than you otherwise would be able to do.

In a shop you can expect most expendable supplies to be furnished. These supplies generally include (but are not necessarily limited to) soap or shampoo, medicated shampoo, cream rinse, dip, toenail polish, ribbons, yarn or bows. Most shops will also provide you with blow dryers, tables, cages and towels. As an employee, you may or may not be expected to have your own clippers, blades, scissors, brushes, combs, mat splitters and rakes.

When applying for work in an established salon, be prepared to answer, in depth, questions regarding dog grooming, your own training, your areas of expertise and previous experience. If you are not especially well versed in some breeds, say so. If you have years of experience show-grooming one or two breeds, by all means mention that fact. Do remember that the salon has a reputation to uphold and will expect you to be able to turn out a grooming job that will reflect well on the shop as a whole. Many owners or managers will expect you to give a demonstration of your abilities by actually grooming a dog. A word of caution might be in order at this point: If your experience has been confined to grooming your own dogs, you may have a real surprise (maybe even a shock) when you have to do a dog as a demonstration of your work. Many of the pet dogs who show up at grooming salons are of questionable temperament at best, and some are downright vicious.

GROOMING FOR A KENNEL

It is a real advantage for a kennel to be able to offer grooming as one of its services, and many kennel owners do not have the training necessary to do the work themselves. The same general rules apply to groomers working for a kennel that offers grooming as a service as apply to those who work for a grooming salon. If it is your intention to do *only* grooming, however, be sure that your prospective employer understands that you are a groomer, not general kennel help. Many boarding or full-service (breeding, boarding, training) kennels hire one person who is expected to wear several hats. It may not be feasible to insist that you will do grooming only if the kennel is a small one with a limited grooming business. You might wish to accept such employment for a period of time in order to get the feel of the business.

GROOMING IN A PET STORE

Like working for a kennel, groomers hired by pet stores are often expected to do other work. In the pet-store situation, this might entail waiting on customers who wish to purchase merchandise, answering the many phone calls received by this type of business or even caring for the animals that are for sale. Here again the experience might be of benefit to you, but if you are planning to do grooming exclusively, you should make that clear from the very beginning in order to avoid a misunderstanding at a later date. Pet stores have great potential for building a thriving grooming business.

VETERINARY CLINICS

A few veterinarians hire someone to work exclusively as a groomer in the clinic. This is not at all common. Most veterinarians hire multipurpose workers who are usually salaried and are expected to act as all-round helpers. Grooming itself forms only a portion of the work that is expected and does not have a very high priority. In general, veterinary clinics have only minimal equipment for grooming and do not have much interest in developing an active grooming business. Frequently, grooming or bathing is simply a sideline and is offered more as a convenience to the client than as a real effort toward building a business in and of itself. In the clinic a high percentage of the groomer's work time will be taken up with simple bath-and-dip clients or with dogs whose owners just want hair cut off either for sanitary reasons, or to help with a parasite or allergy problem, or simply to make the dog cooler for the summer.

You might offer your services as an on-call groomer to come in and work strictly on a commission basis. Make up a portable kit of grooming equipment that you can carry with you. In this way you might be able to groom for several veterinary clinics and find in time that you have all the work you can handle. One major advantage in spending some time working in a veterinary clinic is the opportunity to learn to recognize medical problems so that you can refer your other clients to their veterinarians when the need arises.

This six-week-old Poodle puppy is ready for his first haircut.

With face and feet trimmed, the pup is already much neater in appearance.

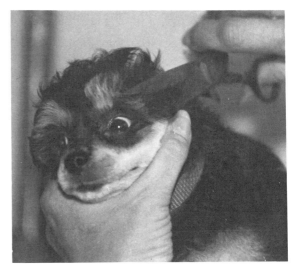

The topknot is shaped with shears.

For a puppy clip, only a light shaping, using shears, is done on the body.

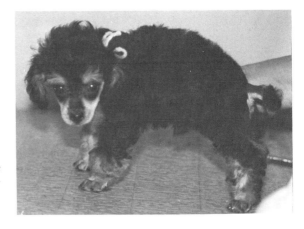

His first clip completed, the puppy wears customer-pleasing little bows.

PROFESSIONAL DUTIES

It would be well to keep in mind that there will be some things you will have to do in any grooming shop, kennel, pet shop or veterinary clinic that do not fall precisely under the title "dog groomer." No matter where you work, you will certainly be expected to maintain standards of cleanliness in the grooming area. This will probably entail cleaning the cages you use to confine the dogs or to dry them, sweeping and mopping the floors, disinfecting and so on. In general, you will be responsible for keeping the area in which you work clean and presentable. A few very large establishments may have someone to perform these tasks for you, but don't be surprised if at least some janitorial work falls to you. If nothing else, you will want to keep your own equipment clean, oiled and serviceable. Learning to keep a clean orderly working area will give you first-hand knowledge of what to expect when you have a shop of your own.

GENERAL HINTS

There are advantages to working as an employee. Primarily, you can avoid the expenses and headaches associated with shop ownership. There are of course, as in any job situation, some areas in which you will wish to be careful. One of the most important of these is being sure of the situation. That is, be sure exactly what your duties will be. Make sure it is clearly understood that you are a trained professional and expect to be treated as such. Naturally, this imposes upon you the necessity to behave always in a professional manner. If you are working on a commission basis, have the terms clearly defined. If you are to be on a salary, be sure you know exactly what duties other than dog grooming you are expected to perform. If you are to receive both a salary and a commission, have those terms worked out in advance. Know ahead of time what equipment, if any, you are to provide. Know what hours you will be expected to work, as well as how many days you will work each week. Know whether or not you are expected to be present at set hours or only during those times when grooming is to be done. Many of the places that hire groomers have at least some weekend hours. Some also will have a few evening hours each week. Find out before you accept the position whether or not you will be expected to work weekend or evening hours. Have an understanding as to who will be responsible for equipment maintenance, blade and scissor sharpening, towel and/or uniform laundry and expendable supplies. Be sure to find out what you are expected to wear to work and whether any uniforms are to be purchased by you or by the employer.

Spelling out all the details in advance will help avoid misunderstandings and unhappiness later. If possible, make a few visits to the prospective place of employment or accept a week's trial period. If you have strong feelings for or against any particular practice (the use of tranquilizers is a good example) be sure that you are in agreement with your prospective employer on that point or points. Once you have accepted employment, there is (or should be) an obligation of loyalty to your employer. In order to have a successful career in dog grooming, as in any other professional field, you must be able to demonstrate your technical expertise, your reliability and your loyalty.

THE OTHER CHOICE

The other major choice you have as a dog groomer is, of course, to open your own business. There are certainly some pros and cons here also.

As an independent shop owner, *all* of the headaches and expenses are yours. It will take time to build your clientele to a profitable level. You may find yourself working longer hours than you would as an employee. An owner simply cannot walk out that shop door at five o'clock and forget the whole thing until eight the following morning. Paperwork may have to be done after hours or on weekends. You may find yourself doing the heavy janitorial work by yourself for a while.

You will soon learn that no one in the whole world will be as involved with your shop and its reputation as you are. You will never find another groomer who cares as much about how your client dogs look as you do. You will never find employees who will be as concerned as you are about how your shop looks, how the phone is answered and how your clients (human and canine) are treated.

There are satisfactions to be gained from starting a business and knowing that you can take full credit for the success of that business. Your income eventually will be greater as a shop owner than it would be as an employee. Within the limits set by your own ambition, you can control the hours and days you work, arrange your vacation schedule to please yourself and enjoy all the benefits of being your own boss. And that folks, is what the balance of this book is all about. A successful business seldom just drops, ready-made, into your hands. In fact, few people would have the knowledge or ability to step right into a successful business and keep it successful if it were a business they had never dealt with before.

As you progress through this book, it is to be hoped that you will be keeping a notebook of the ideas that come to you and that are brought to mind by the things you will read. In some areas, you will find that you are going to need to study books concerned with other specialties. As you learn and study and keep your notes, you will be building your business foundation—a foundation of *information,* and most important of all, *knowledge* of where to look for other information you may need.

2

If I Could Only . . .

Setting Your Goals

Now is a good time to examine your goals, both short and long term, in the grooming business. It is time too, to take stock of your own personal motivations and qualifications for entering this profession.

WHY DOG GROOMING?

If you are considering opening a dog-grooming salon because you think it is easy money, perhaps you should stop right here and now. Grooming dogs for the public can be hard, dirty, thankless and sometimes even disgusting work. There will be days when you will go home with every sort of nastiness on your clothing and the feeling that *you* probably have fleas or ticks by now. Yes, the money is there. Yes, you can cash in on a part of the pet-services industry. Just don't expect the money to fall into your lap and don't expect to make your fortune instantly. Do expect to get out of this business pretty much what you put into it. If you are ready to work, are highly motivated, enjoy what you do and can hold out when things look grim, then you are going to do just fine.

Every shop owner has had the experience of would-be groomers calling or dropping in to make application for work. Usually untrained, these very sincere applicants have decided that dog grooming is the ideal occupation for them because they have no other training and after all, they "just love animals." Don't stay up there on cloud nine. There is a lot more to this business than loving animals. In fact, too much sentimentality can be a real detriment in this work. Certainly, you must like animals to be successful. Absolutely, you must enjoy working with dogs. But you must realize that working with animals also requires strong determination, a strong stomach and a readiness to be physical if necessary. You must also realize fully that at least a fair percentage of the dogs that come through your doors would rather be somewhere else and many of those dogs will not hesitate to make their wishes apparent by biting. If your only experience has been with your own dogs, you may be totally unprepared, and thus vulnerable, the first time a dog makes a serious attempt to commit mayhem with you in the role of victim.

If your sole motivation for opening a grooming parlor is the fact that you have no other training, then you might be well advised to re-evaluate both the situation and your own talents. The owner/manager of a dog grooming business is (or should be) an individual of many and diverse abilities. First and foremost are, of course, the ability to groom dogs and the artistic eye to achieve beauty where little beauty was apparent before. But far more must be expected than that if you are to arrive at your goal of a busy, successful dog-grooming business. How about secretarial skills? Typing and filing certainly have their place in any business and just because dogs don't read hardly makes this particular business an exception to the need for those skills. How about public relations? Who will answer your telephone and greet your clients? Who will write your advertising if you don't do it yourself? No matter what good planning goes into a shop, nothing remains new forever and sooner or later the owner will be called upon to do some handyman-type work, or be forced to call in a repairman at great cost both in time and money. Meeting and dealing with the public on a one-to-one basis is no minor feat in itself. Then, too, you will certainly need a good solid foundation in basic arithmetic—it is important in computing prices, figuring costs and, most fun of all, making your bank deposits. All in all, the owner of a dog-grooming business must, like any businessperson, be well rounded and have a reasonably wide range of capabilities.

YOUR TIME BUDGET

You might benefit by sitting down with paper and pen and making a list of all the things in which you are now involved. This list can guide you in many ways. For the moment, your list of activities can help you in setting your goals as a dog groomer/businessperson. At a later time, your list will be of great value to you in developing your contacts for clientele.

In listing your activities be very detailed. List every little thing that you do. Even small items can be important, whether as a time consuming activity, as a potential client contact, or both. List your household chores, your hobbies (do you have friends who share the same hobby?), time spent carpooling your children (the other children in the carpool have parents, many of the families have dogs and they probably know other people who have dogs), and don't forget any clubs or civic organizations in which you participate. If you do volunteer work, be sure to list an estimate of the hours you work each week. If you presently hold a job, whether full- or part-time, be sure that you list not only your actual hours at work, but your driving time and the time needed for preparation at home. In other words, take a real look at your present life style. From your current list of activities you can begin to form a picture of the amount of time you have available to devote to your grooming business. You may find that simply by budgeting your time more effectively you will be able to continue all or most of your daily activities and still have ample time to begin this new project. If it appears that you do not have enough time, you will have a good detailed list from which you can work in making choices as to which items will be important enough to continue and which activities will have to be curtailed or even cut out entirely. In figuring your time budget, do not neglect to give yourself time to relax. If your time is so tightly planned that you have no time for just plain play then you will soon find that you are deriving little satisfaction from your work.

PART-TIME WORK

Perhaps you only want to work part-time at your new business venture—say two, three or four days per week. When you establish your own business, it is possible to work as few or as many days each week as you wish. The dog-grooming business lends itself well to work of only a few days each week. If you are already employed in some other field of work, you might begin by doing your grooming work only on Saturday or on your day or days off from your present employment. A point of ethics crops up here. If you are currently employed as a dog groomer working for someone else, or if you are employed in any capacity in an establishment that offers grooming as one of its services, it would be a serious breach of ethics, not to mention just downright bad business (and bad manners as well) to start your own grooming shop part-time in direct competition with your employer. This behavior reflects badly on your own ethics and loyalty and can only be damaging to your reputation in the long run. You will find that your reputation will be of great value to you and that people want to entrust their family pet to someone they believe to be honest and trustworthy in every way.

If you are involved in showing dogs (many excellent groomers have learned their trade by preparing their own dogs for the show ring) you will find that your best time to schedule grooming for your clients will be the midweek days. This of course leaves your weekends free to attend dog shows, which are usually held on Saturday or Sunday.

Evening hours might work well for you. You probably will not wish to schedule too many dogs in one evening, but you will soon find that many people would like to have their pets groomed after 6:00 P.M. In fact, this is a real convenience for many people who hold a full-time job and who may find it awkward to get to the doggy salon during regular business hours. In many grooming shops across the country it is becoming popular to open one or two evenings each week to cater to this particular need.

Many women find that a dog-grooming service is a business they can build while still devoting an adequate amount of time to home and family. This is especially true if the grooming shop is located within or adjacent to the home. For mothers with very young children, there is the added attraction of being able to have the children with them at work if they wish to do so. This is an option that is not usually available to an employee. Part-time work is especially appropriate for those beginning this business in their own home. The overhead is kept modest, which allows the business to get on its feet at a more leisurely pace than might be necessary otherwise. A clientele built doing part-time work can be the backbone of a full-time grooming shop in the future.

FULL-TIME WORK

The alternative to part-time work is, not surprisingly, full-time work. For the average grooming salon, this will mean hours from

Mixed-breed dogs make up a substantial part of the business in an all-breed shop, and this shaggy dog certainly needs to be groomed.

This neatly groomed fellow bears little resemblance to the unkempt animal his owner brought to the groomer.

23

8:00 A.M. to 6:00 P.M., more or less. In most cases this will usually prove to be more rather than less. You will almost certainly find that, no matter what your hours, some would-be clients will want you to open early or stay late because your hours don't coincide with their hours or their wishes. It is easy to fall into this trap, but in so doing, full-time work quickly becomes overtime work. As a business owner you can view customer good will as your overtime pay—most customers will resent paying an extra charge for your extra time.

Keep your economic picture firmly in mind before you elect to open your new business full-time. If you have not already built up at least a modest following of clients, your first few months could be very lean indeed. If you are presently working and your family depends heavily on your income you may find that you have imposed a double burden upon yourself. Until your clientele has developed, you may find that your total income has decreased while your overhead has increased, leaving you in a position known euphemistically as a "negative cash flow situation."

Many new businesses fail each year. Of these, at least a fair percentage could have succeeded had the business owner made better plans prior to opening. Others could certainly have been successful given more time for the business to develop. Don't put yourself in this category of "might have been." Plan ahead, be realistic. If anything, overestimate rather than underestimate your expenses. Opening your business full-time right away can mean some lean times early in your career, but if you are willing and financially able to take the risk the rewards can be substantial.

OWNER/MANAGER

It could be you are planning for a large shop employing several groomers. Perhaps you see yourself primarily as a manager. To be successful as a manager with one or more groomers it is necessary for you to be competent as a groomer yourself. Only in this way can you be sure what you can reasonably expect a groomer to be able to do. Even though you don't plan to do the actual grooming work yourself, you will be asked how to do various jobs and it is extremely important that you be able to tell your groomers exactly what you want done and if need be, to show them. Sometimes it is possible for an individual who has the financial capabilities but not the technical expertise to hire as a manager someone who is an expert groomer and who can direct other members of the staff. In general this cannot be considered a practical plan because top-notch managers are not in long supply. We are primarily concerned here with the individual who wants to be actively involved in the operation of his or her business.

If you picture yourself as the owner of a large shop, remember that you will need at least some skills in personnel management. It can be surprisingly difficult to deal with one or more employees if your only experience has been that of an employee. As a manager you will be expected to resolve conflicts between employees, conflicts between employees and clients and various employee problems from tardiness to downright dishonesty. You will soon find that most employees do not have the same devotion to your business that you do. After all, you are the boss. Your employees will assume that you are getting rich on their labors. If you plan to have one or more people working for you and if you have not had much management experience, this might be a good time to think about enrolling in a business-management or personnel-management course at the nearest college or university.

SPECIALIZATION

There will not be a more opportune moment than the present to consider whether you will offer a specialized grooming service doing just one or two breeds (for instance, Poodles and Cocker Spaniels), or if you will groom all breeds. Will you do pet grooming exclusively or are you qualified to offer show grooming in some or all breeds? During this particular phase of your planning, *please* be both realistic and honest with yourself. Far too many groomers overestimate their capabilities in this area and they (or more precisely, their reputation) suffer for it later. If you are trained only in pet grooming, you are certainly not going to endear yourself to a client by doing a pet-type grooming on a dog that client has entered in a dog show next weekend. If you do show grooming on only one breed, then by all means confine yourself to preparing that one breed for the ring and do pet-type grooming on all others. (Your advertising might read "Pet Grooming—All Breeds. Show Grooming for Cocker Spaniels and English Springer Spaniels.") Some individuals do excellent work on one specific breed but are barely competent to do any other breed. By all means, keep on learning and add new breeds to your list as you are able to do so. Your reputation can only profit by your honesty. It is better to do one breed superbly than to do many breeds badly. Remember that you can fool the buying public for only so long. Eventually you will be found out and the only one injured will be you. Many, many groomers around the country make an excellent living through specialization. In fact, in the large metropolitan areas there is a certain snob appeal in taking the family pet to a salon that caters exclusively to that one breed. In this situation, prices are sometimes substantially higher at the specialty salon.

LOOK AT THE OPPORTUNITIES

During this evaluation and goal-setting time period, it would be well to size up the market for your proposed services in your own locality. Obviously, you must think that there is at least some opportunity within a reasonable distance of your location or you would hardly be planning a business of this nature.

By now you have almost certainly checked to see whether or not there are other grooming shops in your immediate area. Or have you? When considering immediate area, think in terms of the shopping radius. That is, do most people in your town or subdivision shop within the actual local vicinity, or do they travel a few miles to the next town or to a more central shopping area for the bulk of their needs? To check, you can run your own survey. It may take a while but in the long run it could pay off. You can conduct this survey by telephone. Simply choose randomly a number of names from your telephone book. Make sure that you have a fair representation from each general part of your town. Call and ask the resident a few simple questions about his shopping habits. Make sure the people you call understand that you are not selling anything. You will find that most people will answer your questions with little hesitation. These questions should be carefully planned to be inoffensive, nonpersonal and informative for you. You might include questions about shopping for groceries, clothing, appliances and specialty items. You may also wish to inquire about shopping for services such as automotive repair, hair care and veterinary care. If you wish to ask whether the family owns a dog and if they currently are having their pet groomed on a regular basis, do so. If a resident does not wish to answer your questions, give them a polite thank you and hang up.

Once you have established a general pattern of shopping habits, you will also have established the radius with which you must be

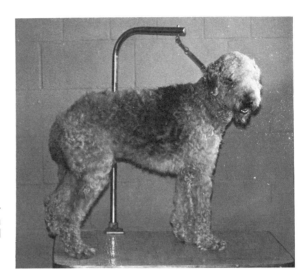

n an all-breed grooming business, you will certainly see a variety of terriers, but most will not be as large as this Airedale.

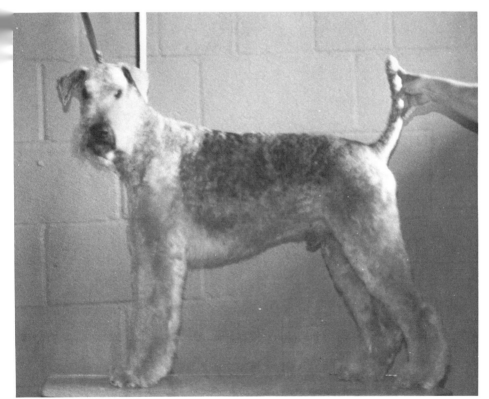

The completed Airedale, like most of the hardcoated terriers, presents a tailored look.

concerned when you check to see whether there are other groomers in the area, and if so, how many. To make your determination reasonably accurate, leave no stone unturned. Call every veterinarian, kennel, pet shop or humane society within the area you will be considering. Scan the newspaper want ads to see if someone is advertising grooming in their home. Make sure that you do maintain a list of all the grooming shops, people who groom at home, veterinary clinics, kennels, pet shops and pounds or shelters for your future use. As you will see, this list will have several applications later.

Maybe you will find that yours will be the only grooming salon in the area. This can have both good and bad implications. Of course, the good is that you will be opening up a brand-new, wide-open concern with little or no competition. Perhaps there will be people who want this service and who have to travel excessive distances to get it. Veterinarians are usually more than glad to be able to recommend a groomer nearby. Right away, you can bet that those veterinarians will send you some clients, and folks who have been driving a long distance will be glad to give you a try. One bad implication to be seen in the lack of groomers in a given area is that this may be an indication that dog grooming is not considered especially important in your particular area. This seems to apply especially in some very rural areas, the general consensus of opinion being "the dawg will just get dirty agin." This kind of attitude can be changed, but it may take a little longer to build a solid clientele in such areas.

COMPETITION

Our free-enterprise system thrives on competition, so don't be frightened away from your goals if you find that there are other groomers in your vicinity. It would be an unusual area indeed if dog groomers had reached a saturation point.

For some reason, dog groomers seem to be a somewhat closed group. There is not as much professionalism nor as much cooperation here as you might find in a comparable group of people involved in some other profession. It may take you a while to become fully accepted by others in your area. Again, don't let this drive you away or make you feel like an outcast. The others have all gone through it, and you can deal with it as well as they can. If there is a local dog-groomers' association, you will probably wish to apply for membership. If there is not such an organization, and if there are a number of groomers within a reasonably small area, perhaps you might try to form something of this nature. A groomers' association can be of major benefit to all its members and to the public as well. This could serve to make you acquainted with the other groomers in your area and could speed up the process of being accepted. Here again, remember to behave as the professional that you are.

By all means, pay a visit to other shops in your area (and in other areas when you are traveling) to introduce yourself, to get acquainted and perhaps to get some ideas for the shop you are planning.

WHAT KIND OF COMMUNITY IS THIS?

In your planning, it is important that some thought be given to the area in which you live. Do you live in a rural area, a small town, a suburban area, a large city, a retirement area? Would you consider the community as a whole to be rustic, high-fashion, aspiring to high fashion, conservative or somewhere between a couple of these general categories? This can have quite a bearing on your decisions regarding decorating your business. It can mean the difference between a shop that radiates practicality and the shop that is definitely high-style.

YOU CAN DO IT

No matter where you live, whether there are a dozen shops or whether yours will be the very first one, you can have a successful business. Dogs are everywhere. Where there are dogs, you will find dog owners who care about their four-legged friends and who want them to have excellent care. You may be surprised to find that some of the toughest, crustiest people will show an amazing concern for their pets, demanding only the best for Rover or Fifi.

In this field of endeavor, you are limited only by your imagination, enthusiasm and goals. If you think you are going to fail, you can bet that you are going to do just that. But if you believe in yourself and in your abilities, if you set your goals high and work toward those goals, you will succeed. Set those goals, evaluate your situation and plunge right in!

3

Can I Afford to? . . .

Financing

WHATEVER YOU DECIDE in regard to the amount of time you will spend in your shop, whether it will be a full- or part-time business, the matter of finances must be considered. Your initial investment can be quite small, just enough for the very basic equipment, or it can be a really large sum adequate to furnish and equip an elaborate shop in a fashionable mall. The choice is yours. The conservative approach may appeal to you, or launching right into big business may be more your style. In any case, the money has to come from somewhere. Sound planning is especially important in the area of financing. The major reason new businesses fail is poor financial planning.

DECIDING HOW MUCH IS NEEDED

How will you determine just how much money it is going to take to get your new business off and running? Those first decisions you made with regard to how much time you will work each week should figure in at this time. Whether or not you have some other source of income will also have a very direct bearing upon the total sum you will need in order to get started. By now, you will have decided whether you will expect this new business to be your sole livelihood from the outset, or if you will be giving it a somewhat slower and more cautious beginning.

A simple formula for determining the total sum needed to start your business might look something like this: basic monthly expenses × 12 + your salary × 12 + initial opening expenses + purchase of all equipment + initial supply of disposable items = first year operating expenses. This can be a shocking sum when you view the total for the first time. Don't panic. This initially staggering amount can very likely be reduced. If, for instance, you do not need to be totally self supporting from the very beginning, you may choose to work without a set salary at the outset. If this is the case, you may eliminate the figure for your total salary, which will substantially reduce the final amount. If you have already purchased your major equipment items, you will be able to drop that amount from the total also.

A few comments are appropriate here in regard to equipment. Very few groomers will find themselves in the position of needing to purchase all of the major equipment items. It would be unusual to find an individual on the brink of opening a dog-grooming business who did not have at least the basic items needed to get started; however, equipment is not an area that can be economized on too heavily. It is important that any equipment purchased should be of the very best quality. Above all, do not be fooled into the false economy of purchasing inferior equipment in an effort to save money. Top-quality equipment will pay for itself many times over. Poorly made equipment not only will break down more easily, but will simply not give the kind of topnotch results you want, and will also cost dearly in lost time. The cheap so-called "pet grooming sets" sometimes advertised for sale are not even really adequate for home-type grooming of one or two pets, let alone for day-to-day use in a commercial situation. Yes, top-of-the-line electric pet clippers are expensive, but when you prorate the purchase price over ten years, the annual cost of owning the very best is infinitely lower than the cost of repeated replacement of inferior equipment. Heavy-duty dryers are expensive also, but will save money in the long run, and in addition have a much better safety factor. Overusing the less-expensive dryers can cause overheating and, possibly, fires. The very best grooming shears on the market will hold an edge and do fine work for far longer than cheap shears. You will be the winner in the long run because you will be able to do your work more quickly (thereby earning more money) and will also save money by not having to have the shears sharpened as frequently. You can see that this is an area where quality will pay for itself, so in planning your budget don't shortchange yourself on equipment. A list of basic equipment plus optional equipment appears in the chapter on interior finishing and furnishing.

Rent and Utilities

One of the major items on your list of expenses will be rental payments or payments on the mortgage for the shop building itself. If you are going to use a part of your home you will not have to include this as an actual cash outlay in planning your initial costs, but will need to add in any special remodeling costs involved. If you are planning to rent or buy, consult with a realtor in your area to get a good idea of the average rate per square foot of floor space. You can then base your rent/mortgage payment estimate on that figure. Explain carefully to the realtor exactly what type of business you are planning to open. Chances are you will thus get a more realistic per-square-foot estimate. Your realtor should be able to give you some very good ideas about spaces available and average costs. You can then get a fair idea of the first-year rental costs. Use one of these formulas to arrive at building costs. If renting: deposits + (monthly rent × 12) = first year total. If buying: down payment + (monthly payment × 12) = first year total.

Monthly utility bills must be figured in as part of your total-cost estimate. Keep in mind that you will be using lots of water and lots of electricity, far more than most businesses. You will also have the expense of a business phone. In most cities a business phone is much more expensive than a private-residence phone. Even installation charges and deposits for commercial utilities are usually a great deal higher than those for private use. In order to determine utility costs, simply call the various utility companies. For the most part, you will find that the companies are very helpful in explaining the various charges to you. A representative will explain the company policy with regard to deposits, installation charges and other initial costs. In some cities, after one year deposits are refunded to you in the form of a credit on your regular bill. In addition, the representative should be able to help you with an estimate of the average monthly cost for a place of business. Again, explain exactly what type of business you will be opening.

To get a really close estimate on the water and electricity, you may wish to double the figure given to you by the utility company. Phone rates will be fairly standard month by month, unless you make long-distance calls. You should know in advance how much your installation will be, plus the cost of any telephones you might purchase, plus the cost of a Yellow Pages ad (this cost will begin with the next issue of the phone book), plus your regular monthly charge. If you live in an area where gas is used for heating and/or for the heating of water, you will also need to get an estimate on the deposit, installation and regular monthly charges for gas.

To estimate your first year's total utility costs, use this formula: total of all utility deposits + total of all installation charges + total equipment costs + (estimated monthly charges × 12) = first-year utility costs. During the first month in business, the utilities can be a staggering outlay. Don't underestimate this and put yourself in a financial bind at the very beginning.

Insurance

Insurance is an expense that is often overlooked. Shop around for an insurance agent with whom you feel comfortable and who is willing to work with you on planning your insurance program. Pick a company for its reputation—not just for its cost. You may wish to do a little research in this area. Talk to others in your area who own businesses. They will usually be more than glad to make a recommendation to you. Remember, you will need insurance to protect your belongings, your building and you. You will need insurance to protect you in the event that one of your clients suffers an injury while on your premises. If you are going to have employees other than yourself, you will also probably wish to check on insuring them as well. In this day and age of burgeoning lawsuits, insurance is an absolute necessity. Don't be afraid to take time to be sure that your insurance agent is covering you in every area in which you will need protection.

Your veterinarian might be a good source of information about an insurance company that will be able to fill your needs because your needs can be quite similar to his. In fact, one phase of protection is called a "veterinary rider." This protection insures you against the loss or death of an animal while that animal is in your care and custody.

Your insurance agent will also be able to advise you about security measures you might wish to take in order to protect yourself against various losses. A really good agent will be more than glad to visit your proposed site and make his recommendations to you.

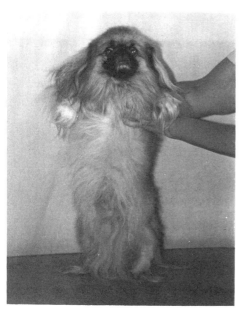

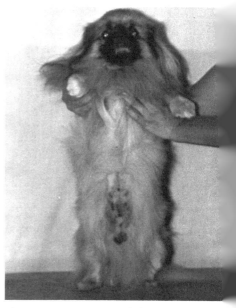

The owners find it difficult to keep this Pekingese clean because he gets dirt and grass in the hair on his abdomen.

The entire area around the sheath and t sheath itself have been clipped clean wit #15 blade.

Show Pekingese should have profuse feathering on the toes—this can be a problem for the average pet owner.

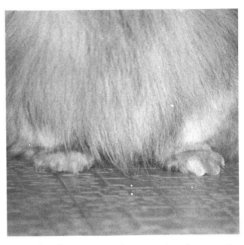

ong hair has been clipped out between the ads and the balance of the hair has been :issored even with the pads.

Long feathering on the toes has been scissored short for easy care.

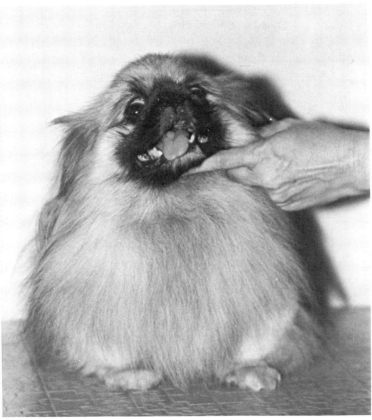

Well combed and brushed, his feet and belly trimmed, this little Pekingese is his owners' delight.

Don't feel that you are imposing on the agent. Don't hesitate to ask questions. Remember, the agent's company would prefer *not* to have to pay a claim, and if the agent can make suggestions that will prevent later losses to the company, he should be pleased to do so. If he is not willing to answer your questions and make suggestions, you might wish to shop further for an agent who seems more interested in you and your business. Let us fervently hope that you will never have to make an insurance claim for any loss, but if you must make a claim, let us also hope that you will have made good plans long before you have to make that claim. Insurance always seems expensive at the time you are working out a plan and it may seem expensive each time you pay the premium. The only time insurance looks like a bargain is when it pays for your loss.

Retail Sales Stock

Whether or not you intend to offer any items for sale in your establishment will affect your total needed cash. Collars, leashes, coats, sweaters, shampoos, flea-and-tick preparations, dog beds and toys are just a very few of the things you might elect to carry for sale. Keep in mind that in order to please your customer you will need quite a variety in size, color, style and perhaps brand name. Even a modest beginning inventory can increase your initial costs at an alarming rate.

If you do elect to have retail-sale items available, you will wish to acquire catalogs from the various wholesalers who are in the business of supplying this type of merchandise. Shop carefully so that you will be paying as low a rate as possible for the items you need. Keep quality in mind as well as cost. You can only hurt your business reputation by carrying shabby items in your place of business. Compare prices and brands carefully. You may find that you want to order some items from one place and some items from another. Beware of accepting merchandise if you are not familiar with the brand name. The wrong merchandise can be an extremely costly error. Some wholesalers will allow returns within a certain time period. Be sure to check the policy of the firm or firms with whom you will be dealing.

Many groomers prefer to carry no supplies at all at the beginning, but become well informed and ready to recommend a store that does carry a requested item. This has the added advantage of building a good relationship with other merchants in your area. Your customers will respect you for your knowledge and helpfulness.

Loan Payments

One very important item to remember in figuring the financial needs of your new business is the payment you will incur by taking out a business loan. Right along with all your other expenses will be a monthly payment to the lending institution. If you have figured your budget closely and have neglected to add in this sum you may find that making ends meet is more difficult than you had projected.

The total payback on your loan will be important to you. To break down borrowing to its simplest form: The longer the note, the more you will eventually pay back in interest. With this in mind, be sure to plan your loan to work to your best advantage. Try to keep the payments within the limits of your ability to pay, but without penalizing yourself by having such a long-term loan that your interest payments are excessive. One way to manage this, if you are personally well disciplined, is to take out a long-term loan and plan to make double payments each month. The advantage is that your payments will be small and, should the unforeseen occur, you can cut down and make a single rather than a double payment. As soon as the crisis is over you can go back to the regular double payment as planned. In this way, no penalty is charged to your account for the month during which you were able to make only the single payment, and during all the months that you make a double payment you are reducing your interest.

To arrive at a realistic idea about loan payments, contact your bank and ask them to give you a sampling of amounts and monthly payments over a particular period of time. This will allow you to gauge fairly closely the amount of your projected loan, and see how it will fit in with your budget.

Projecting Expenses

Now is the time to look at your projected monthly budget and your total opening expenses.

Initial Opening Expenses
Rental deposits or down payment on purchase—
First-month rent or first mortgage payment: _____

Utility deposits (total of all utilities)—
Estimated monthly utility bills (total of all utilities): _____

Purchase of equipment: _____

Insurance: _____

Retail sales stock (if any)—
Supplies (expendable): _____

Subtotal _____

Monthly Expenses
Rent or mortgage payment × 12: _____

Total utilities × 12: _____

Insurance (annual total): _____

Estimated monthly supply use × 12: _____

Monthly salaries × 12: _____

Subtotal _____

Add the above subtotals.

Approximate first-year expense subtotal _____

This figure represents the approximate total amount needed to run your new business for one year, less the loan-payment figure for the working capital. Using this figure, call your bank or lending institution to ask how much the payments would be on this sum of money over a period of one, two or three years.

Loan payment: _____

Loan payment × 12: _____

Now add the subtotal figure to the loan-payment amount that you feel will best suit your needs. This final figure represents the total of yearly operating expenses for your first year of business.

The totals at which you have arrived by using this basic budget will begin to give you a fair idea of the costs involved in opening your new business and in operating it for the first year of its life. Notice that in the monthly-expense section no estimate was given for retail sales stock, because this is an item almost impossible for you to gauge accurately until you have tested your own market.

With the staggering totals in front of you, you are almost certainly wondering by now just how much money you will need to launch your new business venture. Many business experts recommend that you have enough capital at the outset to cover your initial costs plus six month's to one year's operating costs. In actuality, many businesses open each year on far less than the ideal amount. Here again, individuality enters into the picture. How much risk are you willing to take? Are you willing to work for no salary at all and count on the income from the business to support the business from the very first day? If so, then perhaps you will wish to plan only for the amount of cash necessary for the initial opening costs. If you are a more cautious individual, then you will want the security of knowing that the cash is in the bank to help you over those first few months or even the entire first year. If you have already established something of a clientele, then it may be that your needs in the way of cash will fall somewhere between absolute minimum and a generous amount. Only you can decide, but it is certainly a decision that needs careful consideration.

FINANCING

Once you have established a sound idea of how much capital it will take to open your new business, you will be ready to actually seek financing.

If your total figure is low, it is quite possible that you will be able to open on your own resources. This is especially true if you will be starting your new business in your own home, because then you will be eliminating some of the major costs involved in renting or purchasing a business building. You will also be able to greatly decrease the estimated costs for utilities because these are already established in your home and in all likelihood will not require an additional deposit. If you have a comfortable savings account, this alone may prove to be an adequate amount to begin your home-based business on a shoestring basis. If your own resources are not adequate to your needs, then other avenues must be explored.

When thinking of money, most people think first of banks and savings-and-loan organizations. By all means, do look into these possibilities, but check with several and compare costs at each one. They can and do differ. The Small Business Administration is a good source of information on financing for this type of business venture. By all means, write and request they send you their list of publications.

No matter what lending institution you approach, have in hand a full and accurate breakdown of all your expenses. You should also be able to show your projected rates, income potential and any other information that might be even vaguely connected with your venture. Remember that lending institutions are in business to make money too. They must be convinced that you have a firm grasp of the realities of business, and the capability to make your new business a profitable one. Toward that end, a complete resume of your own experience is in order. This lets the lender know that you have the experience upon which to base your estimates. The lender will also want to know about your training (include your licensing if that is applicable in your state), and your current financial position, credit references, personal references and so forth. Essentially, the lender must be convinced that you have the ability to repay the loan you are requesting.

Depending on the size of the loan you are seeking, it may be necessary for you to provide some form of collateral, such as an automobile, your home, land or some other real property to secure the loan. In some banks, it is a requirement that collateral be provided no matter what size loan is being requested.

If you are not granted a loan at the first place you try, don't be discouraged. Ask for a complete breakdown of the reasons for denying your application. Listen carefully, it may be possible to remedy the deficiencies and resubmit the application successfully, or by making the changes noted you may be able to apply at another institution with better results. Again, don't be afraid to ask. Perhaps you have simply chosen the wrong place to apply for this particular loan. The loan officer may be able to offer a helpful suggestion as to another lender who would look more favorably upon your loan application. Be sure to ask whether the application might have been approved for a lesser amount. If the answer is yes, find out exactly how much this particular institution would lend to you on the basis of the application you have presented.

One of your options at this point might be a re-evaluation of the scale on which you have based your original costs. If every lender to whom you have applied has refused your request on the basis of the amount you are trying to borrow, it could be possible that your original plan is a bit too ambitious. Could your plans be revised so that a more modest investment would be sufficient to launch your new enterprise? Perhaps you could open on a slightly more modest scale with an eye toward expansion as your business increases. In your first estimates, have you included needless frills? Can you pare your needs to a figure that might be more realistic?

Recheck every item on your list. Be sure that you have listed all of your needs, but have not gone overboard. If you can re-evaluate your list of necessities and reach a substantially lower amount, perhaps financing will be more readily available. It is almost always possible to expand at a later date, but getting in over your head at the outset could be a disaster. One of your major expenses possibly open for revision is the cost of your location, which will be discussed in the next chapter. There are many ways in which you can pare your costs to a more manageable level. If you have visited many other grooming shops, you have surely seen that there are successful shops operating at almost every level, from very modest in-home businesses to posh salons. Try to be flexible in your thinking. If you cannot maintain a flexible attitude, you will find yourself handicapped in more ways than one.

If all else fails, you may have to accept a job elsewhere and start a savings account with the eventual goal of opening your own business. If this does become a necessity, look at the situation as a learning experience and apply what you learn to your own advantage. If you are working in an office, for instance, you may learn some office methods that later will stand you in good stead in your own business.

Above all, don't be discouraged. If you really want to have a business of your own, set your goals and keep them firmly in your mind. You will be able to achieve your desires.

4

My Little Corner of the World . . .

Choosing a Location

WHEN CHOOSING A location for your grooming shop, a number of options are available to you. You will have to decide whether you will rent, buy, or build, or whether to add to or remodel a part of your own home to serve as your shop. If you do not plan to use part of your present home then you will also have to decide on the area in which you wish your business to be located.

One of the first things you must know, before you can choose your location, are the zoning regulations in your own community. How is a dog-grooming shop classified and how must the area be zoned in order for a shop to be opened? This information is usually available through your city hall or the city planner's office. If the information is not available at one of these two offices, someone in one of the offices should be able to direct you to the information you need. If not, try your city attorney's office. If all else fails, you might have to employ an attorney of your own, but this is highly unlikely.

REAL-ESTATE AGENTS CAN HELP

A real-estate agent can be one of your most valuable allies in choosing a location for your business. Do not hesitate to enlist the aid of a realtor and do not feel guilty about knowing what you want and asking questions. The realtor works for you, remember? Keep an open mind as you look at various properties and also keep a notebook. Look at absolutely anything your realtor might suggest no matter how unlikely it seems. Write in your notebook the address, followed by all pertinent details: the asking price or monthly rental fee, floor plan, any features you especially did or did not like. If you are looking at rental property, be sure to let the realtor know exactly what you intend to do in the way of business and exactly what that entails. He should be able to tell you whether or not the owner will be amenable to your plans. Do not expect the realtor to do all the work of searching out your prospective locations for you. Always be on the lookout for a location that seems to have promise. Note the address and the name of the realtor if a sign is displayed. Then call your own realtor and ask him to inquire about this property. He should be able to arrange for you to see the property in question.

WHAT MAJOR FEATURES ARE NECESSARY

There are several things that will be important considerations to you when thinking about a location for your business. One of the first is accessibility. Your new business isn't likely to get off to a flying start if no one can find your place without a guide. Accessibility is important. You should also think about traffic flow—do lots of people drive or walk past this prospective location each day? What about other businesses in the area? It will be good for your business if there are other well-patronized businesses nearby.

How about the neighborhood in which the property is located? Will your clients be afraid to come into the area after dark? Will they feel comfortable coming into the area at all? During the winter months, your closing time may be after the sun has gone down. If your clients are afraid to come to your establishment after dark because you have located in a bad neighborhood, your business will suffer. Is this an area where you might be afraid yourself? What about the crime rate? If you are unsure, ask other businesses in the area or call the local police and explain why you need the information.

Parking is important to you in choosing your location also. Will you have a place to park? Will your clients be able to park close to your shop? Remember that the client doesn't want to have to lead or carry a newly groomed pet several blocks in the rain because there is nowhere to park closeby.

As a general rule, the better the location, the more expensive it is likely to be. If an older area in your city is being renovated, you might do well to get in on the ground floor, so to speak. By doing so you may be able to eventually boast quite a fashionable address at a minimum cost, so do not overlook this as a possibility. This is especially true if you are planning to buy rather than rent.

USING A PORTION OF YOUR HOME

You may wish to use a portion of your own home when you first begin your business. Many successful groomers have done just that. It can be quite convenient to work from your home, especially if you have a garage or other outbuilding that would lend itself to modification for use as a shop. An unused den or spare bedroom could be made to serve nicely.

When thinking of using a portion of your home for your grooming shop, keep in mind that you will have strange dogs there and their manners may leave something to be desired. Additionally, you could end up with a liberal supply of dog hair throughout the rest of the house if the area you decide upon is not an area that can be effectively closed off from other parts of your home. There is also the very real hazard of bringing in undesirable parasites that may be infesting some of the dogs who come to you for grooming. Once established in your home, fleas or ticks can be a real problem to eradicate.

An attached garage can usually be closed off from the house quite effectively and in addition it will most likely have an outside entrance that could be converted to the grooming shop entrance. This situation allows you very good control over people and animals that otherwise might be traipsing through your living room. The drawbacks of grooming in your home are completely avoided. Depending upon the stage of interior finishing done in the garage or outbuilding in question, you may be able to start your business with little more than the moving in of your equipment.

Naturally the "at home" location will only be available to you if the zoning regulations in your community will allow this type of business in a residential area, or if you are able to get a zoning variance to make yours a special case. If your home is outside the city limits you will need to find out whether county or state laws will make some sort of licensing a necessity.

Grooming right at home can have many advantages at the beginning of your new business venture, the first and most obvious

This house has been converted into a grooming shop and boarding kennel.

being lowered cost. This is especially true for the part-time groomer. Beginning in this way can allow you to build a clientele to support a future, more ambitious undertaking. Being right there at home is especially convenient for mothers who have small children because it allows more flexibility of schedule and virtually eliminates the need for hiring a baby sitter.

One of the disadvantages of having your shop in your home or immediately adjacent to your home is that many times clients will drop in at most inconvenient times to request grooming. Clients seem to feel that since you are there anyway, they can come by at any time. (More about this subject in the chapter on time scheduling.)

RENTING

Another of your options is, of course, renting. It may be possible to rent a building or even a small house in an area zoned for business for a much lower initial investment than purchasing a building. In fact, you may find that you can afford to rent space that would be entirely out of your purchase-price range.

If you choose to rent, do be sure that your prospective landlord is fully aware of the nature of your business and that he has no objection to having dogs on the premises. You will also need to be sure that you will be allowed to remodel or redecorate the space. At the very least, you will need to be able to install your raised tub for bathing, and some landlords might take a dim view of that sort of action.

In looking at rental property, it would be wise to try to find something without carpeting or at least with an entrance area without carpet. Dogs who are thoroughly housebroken at home sometimes backslide the moment they come through the door of a grooming shop or veterinary clinic. In a rented building, you might find yourself in the unenviable position of having to replace the carpeting.

Another rental possibility is a space in a shopping center. If there is a vacancy in a shopping center near you or if a new shopping center is being built, that might be the answer. Keep in mind that although this may be quite expensive to rent, the location may make it worthwhile. In many new shopping centers, the tenants must do all interior finishing. This can mean installing interior walls, plumbing, and wiring and in some cases even completing the front wall of the space as well. Be very sure of the conditions attached to the rental or lease of a portion of a shopping center.

When thinking about rentals, you will also want to think of the terms of that rental. The terms you are willing to accept will of course be entirely up to you, but it might be wise to have some written agreement setting forth those terms. You might choose a lease to help safeguard your cost of rental. In negotiating the terms of rent or lease, your best help can come from your realtor. Your realtor will be able to explain what is meant by the various terms and can also be most helpful in recommending to you the kind of an arrangement that will be most to your benefit.

BUYING

Buying a building or house in an area zoned for business is another of your alternatives. The advantages can be very attractive. After all, if you own the building, you can remodel or redecorate to the limits of your imagination and budget. The only person you will have to answer to will be yourself. You will probably have to obtain a permit from the city for remodeling, but the cost of these permits is usually quite modest. You may also have to have some building items approved specifically, but this is seldom a problem either.

The purchase of a building can be an intimidating idea, but it is after all an investment. If you decide that you no longer wish to remain in business, or if the grooming business does not prove to be as lucrative in your area as you had expected, you will at least have a piece of real estate you can sell, or, if you wish, you will have a building that can be used as a rental property. You might even decide to establish some other sort of business. Purchasing real estate is certainly a long-term commitment and one that should not be entered into lightly, but it is an option definitely worthy of investigation. Again, use the expertise of your real-estate agent to guide you. Your agent has the training and experience to be one of your greatest allies in purchasing a piece of property.

BUILDING

Another possibility you will want to explore is that of building your shop from the ground up. The major advantage here is that you can plan in advance to have the features you would like to have and you can have the building built to suit your own wishes. You will

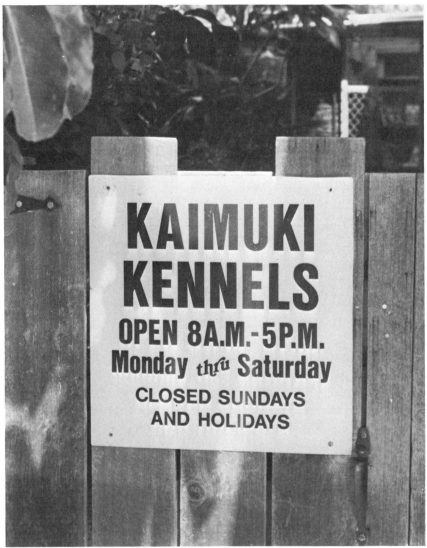

The sign on this entrance makes business hours clear.

certainly want to choose a plan that will give you the conveniences you most desire, and which also will be pleasing to your eye.

When thinking of building your own shop, as always, there will be choices to be made. The same criteria apply to a location for building that apply to a location you would consider for renting or buying.

BUSINESS PROPERTY

Business property in a good location is not cheap and may not be easy to find, but you might wish to make that investment. Prime business property is always a good financial investment. The advantages are easy to see—location has already been considered and zoning is not a problem. Cost may prove to be the only deterrent.

BUILDING ON YOUR OWN PROPERTY

If zoning permits, you may choose to build on your own property. The nature of the building you erect may be dictated to some extent by the city regulations that pertain to building in a residential area, and these can vary drastically in different areas. Some advantages are plain to see, the primary one being that you already have the property, and another being the lower cost of transportation to and from work.

In building on your own property, some of the things you should consider will be these: adding a large room onto your home; building a separate building entirely; purchasing a large portable building and doing only the interior finishing.

In adding a room to your home, you will of course want to plan for your own privacy as well as for convenience. You will wish to arrange a separate entrance for your clients and you may wish to place that entrance as far as is practical from the entrance to your home. It might even be advisable to fence the area so that your private areas are not easily accessible to your customers. Inside this type of addition, it is wise to see that connecting doors into your home are positioned so that they are not readily available to customers. If this is not done, you may find visitors in your home unexpectedly.

Building a separate building on your own property has real

appeal. You will be able to maintain your privacy fairly easily and at the same time you will be quite near your work. Again, separate the entrances to home and business. Placing the business entrance as far as possible from the entrance to your home will discourage to some extent the assumption that you are always on call just because you live nearby. Fencing the business or fencing your home separately will also help to create the illusion of distance that you will soon learn to appreciate. Hedges or privacy fencing can be a great advantage. Remember too that your own pets are not likely to appreciate having a strange dog in their own yard and most of your customers are not as adept at handling dogs as you are. The results could be unpleasant if family pets and customer pets are not kept separate.

Portable buildings provide a functional option for the individual who is pressed for time or who simply would like to dispense with the basic building and get right to the interior work. These buildings come in a wide variety of styles and sizes and can be purchased with the interior completely finished, partially finished, or totally unfinished. The least expensive is usually the totally unfinished type. In figuring costs for this type of building do not neglect to figure in the cost of interior finishing. It would be wise to price these buildings at several dealers and discover the best price. These buildings should come with guarantees on the basic structure, on the treated wood used for underpinnings, on the roof and so forth. Be sure to find out exactly what each company offers in the way of guarantee, delivery and setup. There can be quite a wide range.

If you have a good clear idea of what you want, it is quite possible to have a portable building completely finished to your exact specifications, delivered to the location you have chosen and set up. All that is then left to do is to hook up the various utilities and go right to work. This will not be the least expensive method, but can certainly be one of the most convenient.

One possible way to save money on a portable building is to scout around for a used building. These are sometimes used on construction sites and then offered for sale when the project has been completed. Some portable building dealers will have this kind of building available from time to time, or you might keep a close watch on the classified section in your newspaper. If you find such a building at a real bargain, you will probably be able to find a dealer who can arrange to deliver and set it up for a reasonable fee.

50

TO CONTRACT OR NOT TO CONTRACT

Whether you choose to hire a contractor, act as your own contractor, or even do all the building or remodeling for your business with your own two hands could be the subject for another book entirely. Many good books are available to give you information. A trip to the public library will be most useful to you in making this decision. The more you learn, the better equipped you will be to make this decision.

ANY CHOICE CAN BE THE RIGHT CHOICE

Whether you choose to rent or buy, remodel or build, go for a conventional-style shop or for something quite unconventional, remember that all these options have been put into use by various groomers around the country and all can be done well. Your own needs, desires and pocketbook will help you decide which is best for you. If, for some reason, you cannot have your "dream" shop right now, then plan, study and prepare yourself well for the day when you will be able to start work on the shop you have always wanted. In the interim, get going now on your plans so that you can make your dream happen.

5

How Will it Look?...

Interior Finishing
and Furnishing

DOG GROOMING SHOPS around the country seem to be as individual as the people who own them. Here you are limited only by your own imagination. Even though your finances will have some bearing on how your shop is decorated and furnished, if you use your imagination and are willing to search for good buys, almost any style decor is within your grasp. Perhaps the first thing to remember is that you are going to have to live with your shop and you should be comfortable with the decor. Try also to keep in mind the sanitary requirements of a grooming shop. For instance, a grooming area with long shag carpet might look fine for a while, but trying to keep that shag looking good and free of dog hair will prove to be quite a chore in the long run.

At the outset, try to decide something of what you want in the way of style and what colors you wish to use. Stay flexible in your thinking so that you can adapt your ideas if necessary. With your basic ideas in mind, you will be able to proceed with plans for your shop, making it as individual as you wish. The possibilities are virtually endless. You can be as elaborate as any beauty salon in a fashionable area or as rustic as a country singer or any variation in between. Some shops that cater to a very well-to-do clientele may be downright posh while others may choose to be simple and utilitarian in nature.

One way to get ideas about interior finishing for your shop is to visit as many other shops as possible. If you know someone who has a grooming shop, by all means ask if you might come for a visit at a time when the shop is closed and have a candid discussion about the things the owner does and does not like about his shop. Most owners seem quite willing to share ideas and to give helpful hints. If you are on vacation, try to make time to pay a visit to shops in other areas of the country. Good manners dictate that you call for an appointment rather than just drop in. Groomers are very busy folks and you will soon appreciate how disruptive to the day's work an unexpected visitor can be. If you are not able to take the grand tour of a particular shop because of a time conflict, by all means have a look at the exterior, and perhaps the waiting room or reception area. This can be done without interrupting the groomer at work.

Veterinary clinics are another fine source of ideas for interior finishing. Virtually all clinics will have some sort of waiting area and again you will find that individuality prevails. Most veterinary clinics will also have at least some sort of bathing facility. Some have a full grooming room as well, so do call and ask for a tour of as many veterinary clinics as possible. Most will be quite cooperative if you will explain what you are doing.

Many kennels offer grooming as a part of their regular services. Whether a kennel offers only a simple bath for homeward-bound boarders or full-scale grooming services, you will find kennels a great place to view grooming setups. As with grooming shops and veterinary clinics, always call the kennel in advance, explain that you are planning to open a grooming salon and ask if it might be possible for you to look at their grooming area.

As you begin looking at various places and different facilities, always be sure to ask the owners if they have things that they especially like or things that they have found not to work as well as they had initially hoped. Also, it is a good idea to ask if the owner can refer you to other shops, clinics or kennels that might have a feature that is especially nice. A referral seems to open a lot of doors when you are first trying to put your ideas together.

The more types of grooming arrangements you are able to see, the greater will be your fund of ideas as you develop your plans for your own business. It is unlikely that you will want to copy any one shop or kennel, but you will almost certainly find features that you like in many different places and will want to be able to incorporate those features into your own plans.

When making these information-gathering visits, by all means take notes. If you are adept with a camera, take snapshots of various features. Draw diagrams to help you recall the construction details that you observe. Keep a file of all these items so that you can refer to the information as it is needed. You will be surprised at how quickly you can forget details if you do not make these notes.

FIRST IMPRESSIONS

Remember that first impressions *do* count. Ideally, your client should walk into a reception area of some sort. This need not be a huge area, but should make a statement about your shop. It goes without saying that the reception area will be clean and well lighted. After that, the sky is the limit. This is, after all, your "show" area. Perhaps you will choose to go with a very modern decor such as might be found in a doctor's office. The seating might be benches built right into the wall, with indirect lighting and perhaps just a green plant or two as decoration. Maybe you will choose to have a more homey atmosphere with antique (or junquetique) furnishings, pictures on the wall, a couple of cozy chairs and perhaps a few knickknacks on the shelves.

Do you have a collection of dog figures? Your reception room could be the ideal place to have a display of small sculptures in a wall-hung cabinet or a shadow box. Do you show dogs of your own? Then by all means have a lovely grouping of the trophies and ribbons your dogs have won and perhaps set these off with a wall arrangement of photos taken at dog shows. Your waiting room can also display wall charts of various clips, posters showing dogs in a variety of situations, a rogues' gallery of your clients' dogs or just about any sort of related collection.

If you have chosen to have some supplies for sale in your shop, the waiting area is a good place to have a display case for those items. If you will not have a full-time receptionist it might be wise to have the items on request rather than displayed on open racks.

It is a good idea to be sure that the reception area is basically dog- and child-proof as well as safe. For instance, it would not be smart to have a large poisonous plant as part of the waiting-area decor. (If you don't know what plants might be poisonous, do some studying on the subject. Many of the plants used for interior decoration are dangerous. One good example is the *Dieffenbachia* or Dumbcane.) It would be much too easy for an inquisitive pup to chew on a plant with disastrous consequences. Owners do not pay

In this shop, each groomer has a separate cubicle separated by a half wall from the other cubicles and shop areas.

Glass cases display both merchandise and the owner's collection of dog figurines. In the background are cubicles for the groomers.

much attention to what their pets might be doing (or their children either for that matter) and will surely hold you responsible if an accident occurs.

If the chair you are thinking of using in your waiting area is a family heirloom that could not be replaced at any cost, then you should reconsider its use. It will likely be wet upon, stood upon and perhaps chewed upon before you can save it. If you will be displaying collectibles of some sort, you might want to be sure that they will be on display in such a manner that they will not be swept from the table by a wagging tail or grabbed by a curious puppy.

It is not a good idea to have arriving clients walk right into the actual grooming area. This can upset the dogs being groomed and make the groomer's job more difficult. Should the client's own dog not be quite finished yet, having the owner on the scene can make doing a nice job all but impossible because the dog will be so excited to see his master that he certainly will not stand still. Also, the normal clutter present when work is in progress may not set the best impression in a new client's mind. This is especially true if a toenail has bled or if one of the dogs is making a real fuss over being groomed. Do remember that owners simply do not understand what you are doing. This makes it important that you have a door to the working area that can be kept closed and that is clearly marked "Employees Only," or words to that effect. This may also be important to your liability insurance program because it acts as a safeguard for the customer.

If you will not have a full-time receptionist, you will need to arrange some signal that warns you when someone has come in. This can be as simple as a set of wind chimes or a cowbell on the door, or as sophisticated as an intercom system for the client to speak into. You could also consider an electric bell that is triggered by the opening of the door.

CHOOSE YOUR STYLE

Choose your style and colors and stick to them. The impression you want to make is one of professionalism, harmony and a well-unified atmosphere. This total impression should start at your front door and continue through any area you intend to have available to the public. Some clients will insist on seeing your working area or may just walk on in despite the signs you have posted. This makes having at least the appearance of good organization imperative, and if the reception-area decor can be carried throughout the shop, it will be to your advantage. Naturally, a higher percentage of your decorating dollars will be spent on the more public parts of your shop, while the working areas will tend to be more practical. This does not preclude maintaining your basic color scheme in the working areas. As was mentioned before, the door leading to the grooming area should be clearly marked "Employees Only," "Keep Out" or something that will discourage would-be visitors from disrupting your work. If a client insists upon seeing where your work is done, you might politely but firmly suggest that you will be willing to take him on a tour of the working portion of your shop at a time when dogs are not being groomed. One explanation most clients seem able to accept is that because the client would not want to have *his* dog upset by a parade of visitors while being groomed, it isn't fair to the other clients to have their dogs disturbed either.

FLOOR COVERINGS

Because dog grooming involves dogs who may decide to lift a leg or make a puddle on the floor (or worse), as well as the use of lots of water, soap, insecticidal dip and so forth, and because dogs do shake and liberally distribute these things around, you will want to be sure that the floor coverings you select are easily cleaned, impervious to damage from a variety of sources and waterproof. Essentially, the same criteria should apply to the floor coverings throughout your shop. While the waiting area will not be subjected to usage as severe as that of the working areas, floor coverings should be just as easy to clean and just as durable there as in any other part of the shop.

Wood, Vinyl, Ceramic Tile, Slate and Marble

A good choice for most grooming shops might be vinyl tile or roll-vinyl goods. These are available in a wide variety of colors and patterns and are extremely easy to install. Roll goods have the advantage of being seamless for the most part, which can prevent water getting under the vinyl. The patterns that have a deeply textured surface do tend to be somewhat more difficult to keep clean. When selecting vinyl be sure that you purchase good quality. Often the lesser grades must be replaced at too-frequent intervals, proving to be a false economy.

Hardwood floors are very attractive and can be quite durable. They do, however, require a good deal more care than some other surfaces. Generally speaking, hardwood floors are likely to work out well only if coated with a tough finish and even then may prove to be more trouble than they are worth.

If your budget allows, ceramic-tile floors are virtually ideal. They are much more difficult to install than vinyl, but are also far more lasting. Ceramic tile does not absorb odors, is waterproof and is impervious to most chemicals. The major disadvantage to this floor covering is cost and the fact that it can be dangerously slippery when wet.

Slate or other stone floors, while just as durable as ceramic tile (perhaps even more so), are usually somewhat more difficult to clean because of their irregular surfaces. This does not of course include finished marble flooring, which has all the advantages of ceramic tile, but it would be the plush salon indeed that would be able to boast polished-marble floors. Even so elegant a floor covering as marble does have the one drawback (aside from the expense) that it can be very slippery when wet.

Carpet

Carpet of any sort, including the indoor-outdoor type, is quite impractical in a grooming salon. Hair clings and odors can build up to the point that any effort at cleaning will be futile. The only place for carpeting might be in an office area where traffic will be low and dogs will not be tempted to view the carpet as grass. (Better still, dogs might be kept out entirely.) Even in the office areas, however, hair is still a problem because you will inevitably find that you have carried hair on your clothing or shoes and now have it all over the carpet. Carpeting also has the decided disadvantage of providing an attractive home to some of the same parasites that your clients want to have removed from their dogs. Both fleas and ticks will find a carpet a perfectly delightful place to raise a family, necessitating a visit from the exterminator.

Concrete

Perhaps you already have concrete or are thinking of having concrete floors for your salon. They are certainly durable. Ideally, a smooth finished floor will provide you with the easiest cleaning.

58

Painted concrete floors do look a little better than plain concrete, but also require a bit more maintenance. If you are building from the ground up, you can have color added directly to the concrete before it is poured. This gives a more attractive look and requires minimum care. You might wish to have more elegant floors in your reception area, and with the concrete as a base you can add vinyl or some other surface to make that area more attractive.

WALL COVERINGS

The same basic principles of easy care for floors should apply to wall coverings. One difference is that although walls may be liberally splattered with water, they will not have water standing on them and so need not be as thoroughly waterproof.

Wood Paneling

Wood paneling with a clear waterproof finish is a very practical wall covering in the grooming area, and looks nice. Wood paneling comes in four- by eight-foot sheets and is quite simple to install. The major disadvantage of wood paneling is that unless you are able to locate an exceptionally light color, wood paneling will tend to require extra lighting to compensate for the light absorbed by the darker color on the walls.

Wallpaper

A good grade of washable wallpaper or vinyl wall covering is an extremely practical choice for walls both in the reception area and in the grooming area. The color and pattern choices are very near limitless. You can also use wallpaper in combination with other materials. Wainscoting (a finished wood panel on the lower part of the wall) with a nice wallpaper is very attractive. Wallpaper is not especially difficult to hang and if you wish to do some of the work yourself, you might achieve some savings.

Paint

Paint is one of the most economical choices you can make for wall covering. Paint can be applied over many kinds of surface and can be both practical and attractive. As in so many other areas, select a good-quality paint, because cheap paint can prove to be a false economy. As a rule, cheap paint does not cover as well nor last as long as the better grades. Of course, you can have paint custom blended if you can't find a color that is exactly right. Be sure that the paint you choose is washable. Not all paint is washable and this is a very important feature to you. An exterior-grade paint will usually prove to be more resistant to water splashes and other grooming salon wear and tear than regular interior paint.

COLOR AND ITS USES

Color is going to be important to you, not only for the first impression your shop will make on clients or its decorative function, but also for available light for your work. Although white is the very best possible reflector of light, it can also be the most difficult color to keep looking its best, and smudgy, dirty walls do not make a very nice impression. If white is your preference, think about using an off-white, eggshell or cream shade—the reflected light will be almost as great and smudges won't show so easily. In choosing wallpaper, a small print with a white background is also less apt to show dirt than a plain paper. You will have a bit more latitude of choice in the reception area than in the working areas because the loss of a little reflected light will not be as important there, but cleanliness with minimum of effort will be just as important, if not more so, in the reception area as it is in the working areas.

Any of the whites or off whites will of course lend themselves well to the addition of other colors in your decorating plans. Choose colors that you will be able to live with. Try to imagine the total effect, day after day. It is possible that a thoroughly pink shop might be too much for you although it might suit someone else perfectly. Walls, woodwork, towels, everything, in varying shades of pink will certainly present a unified whole, but not one that most people would care to look at day after day.

Generally speaking, the pastel colors seem to lend themselves well to overall decorating and maintain a bright, airy appearance. The use of a pastel color with either a darker shade of the same color as accent, or a darker shade in a contrasting color as accent can be very attractive. Pastel blue for walls perhaps, with dark or navy blue trim can be very pretty. Light yellow with a bright clear green as trim would perhaps suit you and make your shop bright as sunshine. If walls and background are kept in the neutral ranges, trim colors can be bold and stylish. A cream background with accents of navy and lime sets a modern tone that would be a bold statement. There is no need to be bland in your choices—practicality need not preclude style in any way.

To get ideas about color combinations, you might try looking through mail-order catalogs from some of the large department stores. Often these will show many different coordinating ideas.

WINDOW TREATMENT

Window treatment will of course be dictated to a large extent by the general theme you have chosen for your shop. You will be influenced in your decision if you have the sort of windows that need some covering or decoration. As in so many other areas, you are limited only by your imagination and the practicalities involved. If you have display-type windows you might wish to do some "window shopping" to get ideas for dressing them. Perhaps you will choose to display a stuffed dog or two. It is possible to cut out dog figures from fake fur that can then be styled into various clips. This is time consuming, but quite effective.

If you have a friend who is a good photographer or if you are good with a camera, "before-and-after" photos could make a striking window, or maybe a simple portrait of an immaculately styled poodle would be just the right touch.

Try to let your windows tell your story. Window treatments are so varied as to be almost limitless. Naturally, windows in the working areas of the shop will probably just have shades or blinds, but windows for public viewing are a totally different matter. You might wish to make your window a trademark, something that remains always the same, eye catching and memorable, or you may want to have a window that varies with the season and/or your mood.

The seasonal window needs imagination and constant work to keep it always current, always different, never trite—a window that will cause people to remember your shop and to comment on it to their friends. If you are talented with a brush (a paint brush that is) it is possible to use a poster-type paint and change the window as frequently as you wish.

If you plan to do display-type windows, keep cost in mind and remember also that all of those nice items will have to be stored somewhere or discarded after they have been used. Dogs can fit into almost any seasonal theme, so you shouldn't have any trouble

A restaurant dishwashing hose assembly is durable and allows water to be adjusted and left on without risk of damage to the hose. The center mounting makes it possible to reach either end of the tub.

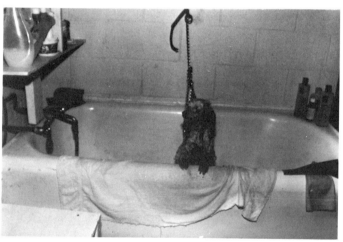

An eyebolt attached to the wall allows the groomer to secure the dog in the tub.

finding something to suit you that will be different from any other window in town.

If you will be selling supplies in your shop, these can make a most attractive display window that will let passersby know that you have retail items available.

THE WORKING AREAS IN YOUR SHOP

As you move from the front or public portion of your shop to the working area, three words tell the whole story: clean, practical, attractive. The first two are critical. As was mentioned in discussing your reception area, floor coverings and wall coverings, washability is of utmost importance in any grooming establishment. Especially in the working areas, floor surfaces must be of the sort to take endless scrubbing without suffering harm and should be of a smooth nature that will not trap dirt. If your budget is limited even smooth-finished, unpainted concrete floors will suffice. By all means, try to keep floor colors light in order to help the entire area retain a light atmosphere. As you know, in grooming good lighting is essential and large expanses of dark surfaces, such as floors or walls, tend to absorb the light that is necessary and make the working area both difficult to work in and depressing. Whether you intend to carry your basic color scheme through into the working portion of the shop will be your own decision. It certainly makes for a unified appearance if you choose to do so, and if any of the working area is partially visible from the reception area it is important that your general impression be carried out.

Bathing Area

When you are planning your grooming shop, there are many ways to cut corners without any sacrifice in quality. A good example is in the cost of your bathtub. This is, of course, one of the essentials in any grooming shop and a tub can be quite expensive. The cost of a new bathtub is high especially when compared to the cost of a used one. If you are willing to take your time and look around, it is usually possible to find a used bathtub at a tremendous savings. It is not unheard of to find a used tub for as little as ten percent of the cost of a new tub.

Some sources for used tubs are salvage yards, surplus stores, contractors, plumbing supply stores and junk dealers. These are also good places to look for the necessary hardware to accompany the tub for use in bathing dogs—the sort of nozzle used in restaurant kitchens for dishwashing is hard to beat. Another type of nozzle you might want to look for is the sort used by beauticians to shampoo hair. Again, check the same places for this kind of used item.

It helps to keep your eyes open and to alert friends that you are in the market for used plumbing items. Mention all the things you need when you call various places to ask what they have. If one place doesn't have what you need, by all means ask if they know who might have it. Perhaps someone is doing some remodeling and would be glad to have you take that old tub off his hands for just the cost of hauling it. A chip or two here and there won't make any difference to the dogs and can easily be repaired with one of the liquid products made for that purpose.

You will want your tub raised for bathing convenience and two economical ways to do this are by the use of concrete blocks as a base, or by building a frame of heavy lumber. In either case, the tub area can then be enclosed with sheets of formica and the end result is most attractive as well as being quite practical. If you wish, arrange doors in the enclosed area below the tub so that this can be used for storage purposes. This is also convenient should you ever need to gain access to the plumbing beneath the bathtub.

An antique tub on claw feet is a charming addition to some shops and most of these tubs have the advantage of being deeper than modern bathtubs. These tubs are somewhat more difficult to enclose than the more modern tubs, but it can be done, or you might choose to leave the tub exposed so that it becomes a decorative accent.

If you will be doing only small dogs in your grooming shop, you might wish to look at some of the small portable tubs on legs sold by several of the large department stores. These are usually sold to be used in laundry rooms and have a drain on the bottom that can be closed or opened with a valve. While quite small, these can be perfectly acceptable if you do not intend to do large dogs. They could also serve as an auxiliary tub if you are very busy, or could be used exclusively for dipping animals for parasites.

Lighting and Electrical Outlets

Lighting and the availability of electrical outlets will be of great concern to any groomer. If you have elected to build your own shop, you will be able to plan these items right from the beginning to exactly suit your needs. If you are remodeling a building, generally you will find that the existing lighting and electrical outlets are not adequate for your business.

Probably the least expensive and most satisfactory lighting for the price are ceiling-hung fluorescent fixtures. These are relatively easy to install and provide the bright yet glare-free light you will find essential for your work. The fixtures designed for use in home workshops are quite inexpensive and are hung from adjustable chains so that the lights may be installed exactly where you want them. When using this type of fixture, be sure that it is hung high enough above the grooming table that it will not interfere with the groomer at work, and so that a dog who stands on his hind legs on the table (even a large dog) cannot reach the light fixture.

Another way to supplement the lighting is to install a clamp-on light either on the grooming table itself or on the wall behind the table. The type of lights used for drafting tables are adjustable, jointed and some have a magnifying glass in the center of a circular fluorescent bulb. The magnifying glass can come in handy when cleaning out ears or doing other very close work. These fixtures are somewhat expensive, but can often be found at a reasonable price if you will check military-surplus stores or auctions.

In any case, err on the side of too much light rather than too little. By all means have the lighting set up on several separate switches so that you need not turn on all the lights if they are not required. It is much easier to turn excess lights off than it is to work with insufficient light.

Electrical outlets may present more of a problem than lighting. In an older building, extensive rewiring may be necessary and this will certainly call for the hiring of an experienced electrician and may also require a special permit from your city.

It is usually most satisfactory to have a row of outlets running the length of the grooming room in intervals on each side. You will be the best judge of the number and location of outlets that will best serve your own work requirements and the dimensions of your grooming area. Again, if you are building your own shop building, this will be planned long before the shop is completed. If this is the case, plan more than enough outlets for now, as well as for any expansion you might wish to make at a later date. It is almost impossible to have too many electrical outlets, but it is very possible to have too many of them on one circuit, so be sure that the outlets are on several circuits rather than just one or two. In an older building, it may be most practical to simply install a conduit on the outside of the wall for outlets rather than to have to tear into the wall and do a complete wiring job. For safety's sake, be sure that the wiring you plan is more than adequate to carry the load, not only for now, but for increased load in the future as your business increases.

Remember that those heavy-duty dryers use lots of electricity and that you will be using more than one of them at a time. Try to make a complete explanation of this to the electrician who is doing your wiring for you. Some electricians will think that you are exaggerating your electrical needs. If necessary, insist that the wiring be made far more than adequate. It is much less expensive to have it done at the beginning than to have it done over at a later date as your needs increase.

Storage Space

Storage space in a grooming shop can become a real problem. One of the most economical and practical forms of storage is simply open shelving. It has the advantage of being easily installed as well as inexpensive, and is very flexible in its uses. Shelves can be used to store bulk amounts of shampoo, dip, cream rinse, as well as clean towels, dispensers for shampoo and extra supplies of all sorts. Shelves can be installed in what might otherwise be waste space—in corners, behind doors or wherever a small area is available. A long shelf over your bathtub or at the end of the tub can hold all your necessary bathing supplies within easy reach.

Shelves can be as simple and inexpensive as a system of brackets with various-width boards resting upon them. Another way to build simple sturdy shelves is to use brick or concrete blocks as supports. This type of open shelving will hold great weight and has the added advantage of being easily moved or rearranged if your needs change.

Another form of open shelving that is far more elegant and professional in appearance (and much more expensive as well) is the stainless-steel baker's rack used by commercial bakeries. These are easy to clean, move easily on their wheels and will stand up to all manner of hard use. They can be obtained from a restaurant-supply store.

The major disadvantage to be found in open shelving is that

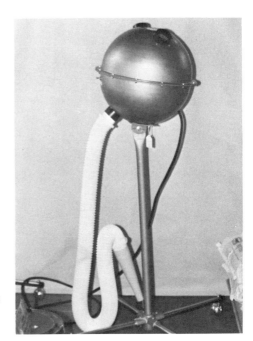

A stand-type dryer with a flexible hose and nozzle.

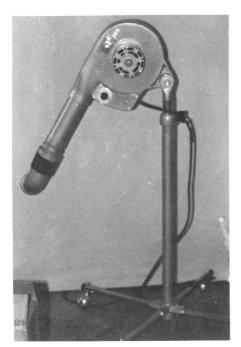

Stand dryer with a rigid nozzle instead of the flexible hose. This allows the groomer to have both hands free.

This table-model dryer is equipped with hooks on the base that allow it to be used as a cage dryer.

The table dryer being used as a cage dryer.

This cage dryer cannot be used as a table dryer. Note that the dryer is being used with an airline shipping crate. When using this type of cage for drying, it is important to be careful not to overheat the dog.

hair and dust will accumulate there, making frequent cleaning necessary.

Closed-cupboard storage, while more expensive, will require less cleaning than open-shelf storage. Cupboards can range from simple home-built units to the most expensive chrome-and-glass units, available through medical- or veterinary-supply houses. You might wish to look at the enamel-on-metal kitchen cupboards that are sold by most large mail-order houses. These are available in a wide range of styles and sizes. Some are wall-hung units and some are free standing. They are midrange in price.

Another form of shelving is of course kitchen cupboards that are sold in units to fit every need. You can virtually custom design any sort of storage you might desire and can plan for as much or as little ornamentation as you wish.

Storing Your Grooming Equipment

Your grooming equipment is the foundation of your livelihood, and it must be well cared for and stored where it will be safe and conveniently at hand.

A simple drawer on the grooming table can hold most of the hand tools necessary to the groomer's work. Some grooming tables come with such a drawer built in. These allow the groomer to keep scissors, brushes, combs and extra blades right where they are needed. If this is your choice, use a silverware tray (plastic or rubber) to keep the drawer well organized so that tools can be located easily.

A pegboard installed on the wall behind the grooming table (or to one side) with one or two shelves above it is versatile and can adapt to a wide variety of equipment. A large portion of the equipment you will be using can be hung on the pegboard within easy reach and every item is easily seen. The shelf or shelves above can hold spray bottles, clipper cooler or anything else you might need that cannot conveniently be hung on the pegboard. A clipper holder can be mounted right onto the pegboard.

Some groomers have automatic cord reels suspended from the ceiling to hold their electric clippers. These reels keep the clippers safe from being knocked to the floor, yet within easy reach. Blades may be mounted on a special holder that has a magnetic trip to secure the blades. It is also possible to purchase the magnetic strips at a hardware store and to install them in any fashion you might find convenient.

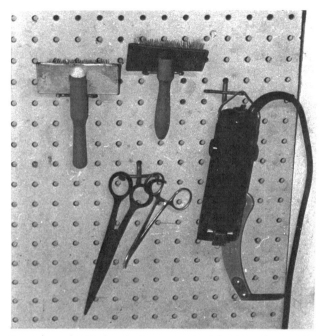

A pegboard with hooks is convenient for keeping equipment within easy reach.

Even something as simple as headless nails driven into a board will provide a place to hang equipment.

A cord reel keeps clippers hanging safely out of the way and extends for use.

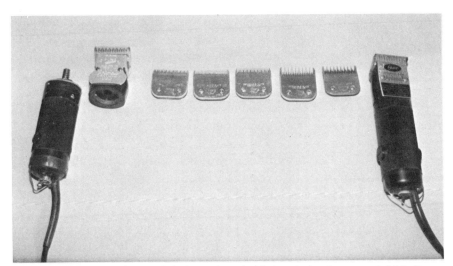

The Oster model A2 clipper (left) has a detachable head, the Oster model A5 clipper (right) features clip-on blades.

If you plan to use a pegboard setup, be sure to measure the height of installation based on your own grooming habits. If you customarily sit to groom, your pegboard will need to be a bit lower than it will be if you do all your work in a standing position. When making the measurements for the installation of the pegboard, the height of your chair and the height of the table on which you normally work should also be taken into consideration.

Crating

Another item of furnishing that will be absolutely necessary in a shop situation is some sort of crate space for the dogs who come in to be groomed. Any number of arrangements can satisfy this particular need.

One way is to build your own bank of crates, using lumber and wire in any combination you find convenient. Home-built crating serves many groomers quite well, but be aware of some of the disadvantages. If built of wood, this type of crating can be less convenient to keep clean, and will absorb odors, dirt and oils from those dogs who arrive in bad shape. If you choose this type of crate setup, you would be well advised to seal the wood with one of the clear polyurethane-type finishes. This will last for years and will help keep the crates clean and odorfree. Another alternative coating is fiberglass rosin. This is extremely hard and durable. You might also consider the use of white formica on the inside of the crates. The surface is smooth and easy to clean and if properly installed should prove effective.

When finishing the interiors of home-built crating facilities, try to make the finish as light in color as possible (such as the white formica mentioned) because this makes it much easier to see into the crates and check on the occupants. If you use a white paint on crate interiors, be very sure that you do not choose any paint containing lead.

One advantage to building your own crating is that the crates can be custom fitted into the space available. Sometimes, making each crate just one inch narrower will prove a substantial overall saving in space.

There are many manufactured crates on the market in a wide price range. When purchasing crates, beware the false economy of purchasing the least expensive ones. Some of these crates are sold by two of our largest mail-order stores. These particular crates tend to lack durability and, worse yet, are not safe. Some crates are so poorly constructed that it is possible for a dog to squeeze its head through between the top and the front panel of the crate, which creates the very real hazard of the animal being choked to death. Be sure to check the construction of any wire crate you might wish to buy. There are some wire crates that have an overlap so that the animal inside cannot get a head or leg out through the joints between the front and top of the crate. These crates are much more safe to use.

One excellent choice in crates for a grooming salon are those sold by the major airlines for shipping. These crates are made of heavy plastic or fiberglass and are easy to clean, odorfree, safe and moderately priced. They come in a variety of sizes and can be stacked quite efficiently. Should you elect to buy this type of crate, do make an effort to purchase directly from the airlines. They are able to sell these crates at a very reasonable price due to bulk purchasing. Airline-type crates are available through retail outlets, but these are usually substantially higher in price.

All-metal crates are also available. These are usually made of sheet aluminum and are durable and easy to clean. They do tend to be expensive. Another disadvantage is that the aluminum will tend to discolor white or very light-colored dogs.

When thinking of all-metal crates, the very top of the line in crates or cages for a grooming salon is the stainless-steel cage of the type most veterinarians use in their clinics. These come in modules that can be used free standing or built-in, and additional units can be added as the need increases. These stainless-steel cages are the ultimate in easy care because there are no seams inside to collect hair, dirt or other particles. A wipe with a damp cloth will keep them clean and odorfree. The latches are secure and the cages are virtually escape-proof.

Stainless-steel cages have only two disadvantages. One is their lack of ventilation, which can cause a dangerous accumulation of heat when dogs are being dried in the cages, and the other is price. The stainless-steel cages are the top of the line in price as well as in quality.

If your budget allows, by all means have the very best. Stainless steel cages will last a lifetime and still be in perfectly good condition.

One way to cut corners on your cages or crates is to keep close tabs on the thrift stores, junk shops, yard sales and classified ads in

This custom-made bank of cages is constructed of welded pipe and chain-link mesh.

A long wall accommodates three levels of home-built wood and wire cages. The largest cages are on the lowest level, which eliminates lifting large dogs to an upper cage. The area above the cages provides storage room and a place for potted plants.

The inside of this cage is lined with vinyl floor covering to make cleaning easy.

your area. People frequently sell crates far below retail price just to avoid storing them. You might even consider placing an ad in the local paper stating your willingness to buy used shipping crates.

If you have a large airport near you, check with the various airlines to see what is done with crates that are left at the baggage department. People who have small cars sometimes simply remove an animal from the cage in which it was shipped and abandon the crate on the spot.

The Overheating Hazard. A word of caution is appropriate about the use of completely closed cages for drying dogs. Be very, *very* careful that the cages or crates you will be using for drying dogs have more than adequate ventilation. It is all too easy to make a crate into an oven with all that hot air pouring in from the dryer. Dogs have been killed this way. Crates should have ventilation on all four sides if possible and at the very least should be open on the front (wire mesh is fine) and have plenty of ventilation at the back. If you are using some of the plastic airline crates, it is no great chore to drill some extra holes for ventilation using one of the small saws made to drill round holes for the mounting of door knobs. These are inexpensive and mount on a regular power drill. This could be one of the most valuable modifications you can make on your crates.

Grooming Tables and Arms

A well-constructed grooming table is the dog groomer's best friend. The grooming table allows the dog to be positioned at a comfortable working height and confines his movements so that the groomer is able to work without having the dog leave the area.

Grooming tables can be purchased from a number of commercial sources. If purchased commercially, a grooming table can be quite an investment. Tables come in a variety of sizes and heights, with and without an equipment drawer and mount for a grooming arm, but all the commercially made tables have one thing in common—they are expensive. One of the best alternatives to the high price of commercially built grooming tables is to build your own. This is easily accomplished even if you are not a carpenter.

The majority of grooming tables are built with the type of folding legs most commonly seen on banquet tables. These legs are available from some of the large mail-order department stores and may also be found in some hardware stores. The legs come as a set of two, which means two sets are enough for one table. These legs are mounted with bolts that are inserted from the top of the table and are secured on the bottom with a washer and a nut. The head of the bolt should be countersunk in the table top. Countersinking simply means that the head of the bolt goes into the top of the table so that it is level. For instruction on countersinking, check any book on carpentry for beginners. If you are unable to find such a book, ask one of the employees at your local lumber store.

The top of the grooming table should be made of 3/4-inch-thick plywood. Do *not* use fiberboard, because it will sag after a while. The size of the tabletop is dictated by your own preferences and by the width of the legs you will be using. A common size for grooming tables is 24 inches wide by 36 inches long. The corners of the top should be rounded off neatly.

To cover the tabletop so that the wood is protected and preserved can best be accomplished by the use of roll-vinyl goods such as might be used on a floor. Remnants are usually available at a very reasonable price. The vinyl should be secured to the plywood with a good adhesive. The edges can then be finished with the sort of flexible aluminum molding that is sometimes used around counter-tops. This is available at most lumber and hardware stores and is secured with screws. If the corners of the table have been rounded, this molding will bend smoothly around the corners, allowing the entire table to be done with only one strip of molding and leaving no sharp edges at the corners. Begin installing the molding strip in the middle of a side rather than at a corner.

When choosing materials for a grooming table, you can save a bit by purchasing a lesser grade of plywood. It doesn't have to look good because it will be covered with vinyl. (Do not make the mistake of using indoor-outdoor carpeting on your tabletop. It is impossible to keep clean.)

The end result when building your own table can be a very satisfactory grooming table at a great savings in cost.

A grooming arm is your third (and maybe your fourth) hand when grooming dogs and it must be solidly constructed. There are two basic ways to attach a grooming arm to a table. One way is to cut a hole in the table and mount the grooming arm in a flange that is tightened on a grooming area with a set screw. This is a very strong and stable mount. The only disadvantage is that it is permanently positioned and cannot be moved. The second way to mount a

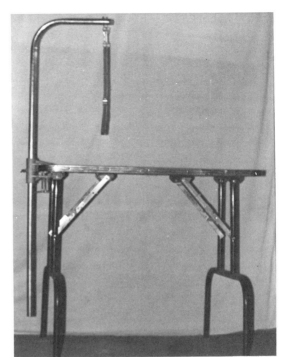

This grooming table is home-built, using banquet-table legs that can be folded flat. The grooming arm clamps on the table and is extra long to accommodate most breeds.

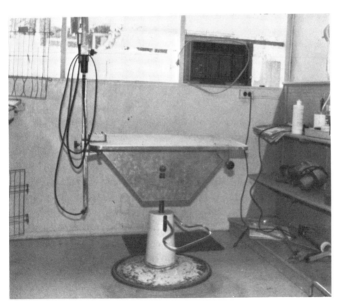

Hydraulic tables like this one are convenient but expensive. This model is equipped with a built-in motor-driven clipper.

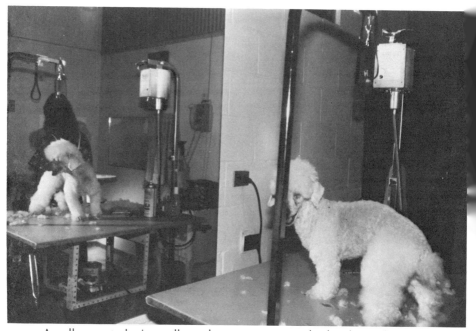
A wall-mounted mirror allows the groomer to see both sides of the dog.

grooming arm is to use the kind of grooming arm that comes with a clamp-type mounting. The mounting is secured to the table top with a clamp that is attached to the side of the table. The grooming arm then slides into the hole in the clamp and is adjusted by means of a wing nut or set screw. This type of arm can be moved from place to place on the table if need be.

Grooming arms are best purchased from a reputable wholesaler. Look at several types if possible before you order your own. A poorly constructed grooming arm can bend if subjected to too much pressure. The sort of grooming arms offered to the general public from some department stores are *not* adequate for use in a commercial situation. The difference in price between the poorly constructed grooming arm and the well-made commercial-grade grooming arm is not great.

It is possible to contrive a grooming arm from various pipe and fittings, but the result will not be satisfactory. Some groomers also use a heavy-duty bracket attached to the wall (the type used to hang plants), and then simply secure a nylon lead to this bracket. This can serve the purpose, but is more or less permanently mounted, which means that the table must remain in the same place and, additionally, must be quite close to the wall.

Generally speaking, you will find that a well-constructed grooming arm is a good investment and will more than pay for itself in convenience.

YOUR DAY-TO-DAY WEARING APPAREL

Although this chapter is primarily about the interior finishing and furnishing of your shop, what you wear to work is, when all is said and done, a very real part of the general impression made by your place of business. Since you are to a degree in the public eye, it hardly needs to be said that your choice of work clothing will need to be neat, clean and attractive. Few things can spoil an otherwise good first impression as quickly as a grubby, sloppy-looking groomer. By contrast, a neat, clean, crisply uniformed groomer sets a truly professional tone. You will have devoted many hours to creating just the right "look" in your shop, don't let a careless personal appearance hurt your business.

Certainly, groomers work hard. This can be a hard, dirty job and many dogs will come to you in filthy condition and they may be covered with parasites as well. This is still no excuse to look unkempt. A neat hairstyle; tidy practical working clothes; clean fingernails (ladies, chipped nail polish is worse than no nail polish); a light touch with make-up, if desired; shoes that are comfortable and clean—all these things add up to the professional image you wish to project. This is the image that will instill in your clients confidence in you and in your abilities. A dirty groomer, with dirty hair and filthy clothing certainly makes a statement about the shop, but it is not the kind of statement you would want to have made.

In choosing your working clothing, remember that you are a part of the overall impression made by your establishment. If you consistently wear the same colors, then this becomes your "uniform" and quickly identifies you and other employees (if any) as part of your shop.

Uniform jackets are a practical choice for the grooming salon. Keep in mind that while crisp white cotton or nylon jackets look great when you put them on, they tend to get dirty easily and may look messy early in the day. Don't forget that a trimmed toenail might bleed or a dog might have mud (or worse) on his feet. Imagine the impression you will make on your clients if you come to the reception area looking as if you worked in a slaughterhouse. If white is your choice, be sure that you keep an extra jacket or two handy for needed changes. Some groomers choose to further cover themselves with a plastic apron while they are working. This does provide some protection for your clothing and from the irritation of hair working its way through the fabric of your jackets. A plastic apron can help keep your clothing dry when you are bathing dogs, but plastic can also tend to get hot. You will have to weigh the benefits against the drawbacks for your own comfort and convenience.

Uniform jackets come in so many styles and colors that you should be able to find something that will please you. A pretty pastel print or a nice bandanna print will hide smudges well and will keep you looking fresh longer.

Jeans are an excellent choice for wear in most shops. Durable and comfortable, jeans have the added advantage that dog hair won't cling to them, and any color or pattern jacket or smock will look good with them. A pair of well-fitting jeans will stay neat looking all day. If jeans are just not for you, then choose slacks or a comfortable skirt that will keep you looking your best.

Another possibility is to choose a uniform dress and then use a smock as a coverup to keep the uniform clean. Some groomers like this because they can slip the smock off before going into the reception area and be sure that their uniform is clean.

For ideas about uniforms, grooming jackets or smocks, check uniform stores and the specialty catalogs from the well-known catalog-order stores. There are many places to purchase uniforms. If you are unable to locate such a store or catalog, drop by your local hospital, doctor's office or veterinary clinic and ask someone there where they get their uniforms. They will almost certainly be able to steer you in the right direction.

You will be pleasantly surprised to see the wide variety and stylish designs available for both women and men. Uniforms have seen some real changes in style and comfort.

Another option for the groomer is to subscribe to a uniform service. These services will provide you with a specified number of clean fresh uniforms each week. They will also provide laundry service. What this means is that there is no need to worry about washing your uniforms or smocks, and you can count on having fresh uniforms available at all times. You may find that your selections are more limited if you choose to have a uniform service, however.

Some uniform services can also provide a towel service if you so desire. This is a real convenience for you and you need not worry about doing the laundry so often because the dirty towels simply go to the service and you are provided with bundles of clean fresh towels each week or each day depending upon your needs. The uniform and towel service can be a great convenience. It can also cost money, so be sure that the time saved is worth the money you will spend.

Whatever your choice in uniforms, let it be something complementary to the basic theme in your shop (if your shop is Western rustic, how could you choose anything other than a red or blue bandanna print?), complementary to you personally and generally professional in appearance. Be sure that you check the materials carefully because all fabrics do not shed hair equally well. A few samples from a fabric store will allow you to experiment and learn for yourself which textures are best.

Rest assured that all the thought and care you put into the appearance of your shop and into your own professional appearance will pay off in the long run.

6

Tell the World . . .

Publicity Builds Business

AS WITH VIRTUALLY any business, in order to succeed, the new grooming salon must in some way make itself known to the prospective client. This is especially true if the business will be opening cold—that is, with no clientele built up from work done at home or in another grooming establishment.

WHAT'S IN A NAME?

Even before you can begin to advertise, you must choose a name for your business. Must it be said that you will wish to select a name that will still be appropriate and palatable in five, ten or twenty years? In this area, use your creative skills and imagination to develop a name that will be memorable, original, easy to pronounce (and spell), not subject to ridicule and not suggestive or vulgar. The obvious (though not terrifically original) could be as simple as the use of your own name. For instance: "Mary's Dog Grooming," or "Smith's Grooming Salon." If your business is a partnership, perhaps you will wish to make a play on the names of the partners. If Ann Smith and Nancy Gold owned a grooming shop it might be called "Goldsmith Groomers," or "Nancy-Ann's Fluff Shop." Here is a short list of names to help start your imagination working: The Clip Joint; The Dog House; Roomin' n Groomin' (offering both boarding and grooming); Pat's Poodle Palace; Bark n Purr (for both dogs and cats); Karisma K-9 Center (all services for dogs); The Pet Stop; The Pampered Poodle; The Pampered Pet; Hair Apparent.

With a little imagination you can develop a name with all the provocative qualities you want. At the same time that you are choosing a name, you may wish to design or at least develop ideas for a logo that will help make a statement about your place of business, or that will make the name more memorable. As an example, a shop that was called *The Pet Stop* had the word *Stop* enclosed in a red traffic stop sign. This is a most distinctive emblem and one that people remember. *The Dog House* might show a simple dog house outline with a well-groomed dog peeking out and the name arched over the door.

Toss around all sorts of ideas for names and logos. Try your ideas out on your friends, try writing them out, try them out by telephone. Trying out your prospective business name by telephone may sound silly, but it will help you choose a name that is not difficult to understand over the telephone.

If you have an idea for a logo but do not have the artistic ability to complete the design, you may need to seek the services of an artist or designer. Keep in mind that this name and this emblem will be the face you will be showing to the world in all of your advertising for many years to come. Be sure the name you choose is really the name you want.

PAID ADVERTISING

Advertising falls into two basic categories: paid and free. When it comes to paid advertising, your only limits are your budget and your good sense. Heading the list in paid advertising is your ad in the Yellow Pages section of your telephone book. Although relatively expensive considering the cost of each ad and the once-a-year printing, a Yellow Pages ad is still a good investment. By all means, take out an ad in the Yellow Pages and make that ad as distinctive as possible, and as large as you can afford. If your telephone company allows you to choose the placement for your display ads, ask to have your ad on the same page where the heading begins. Also, when selecting multiple listings (that is, other categories where you want your name to appear, such as Pet Services or Dog Grooming), be sure that you are not listed with Pet Shops. If you are listed as a pet shop, you will be kept busy with questions such as "How much

This large logo is eye catching, and its location on the building facade makes it easy to see.

An expanded form of the logo is shown on the front window of the shop.

are your gerbils?" and "Do you have any kittens for sale?" These calls can become a real annoyance and can keep you occupied with the telephone when you could be doing more profitable work.

Most telephone companies will have advertising design people to help you in planning your display advertising. Do of course incorporate you own logo in the ad. Insist on seeing a proof copy of your ad before the telephone book goes to press. It is especially important to be sure that your ad is correct in the Yellow Pages because the telephone book is only printed once each year and whatever is printed you will have to live with until the next telephone book comes out. Check all pertinent information very carefully, making sure that every single detail is correct. It can really be a problem to have your address listed as North 10th Street when in fact you are located on South 10th Street. This is a tiny error in terms of ad appearance, but a possibly costly error in terms of helping prospective clients locate your place of business.

Next on your list of paid advertising will be the communications media. This includes television, radio and newspapers. Television may prove to be prohibitively expensive for the small business; however, if you feel that you can in fact afford a few television "spots," let the television station professionals help you to plan and produce them. Don't feel that it is imperative for you to star in your own advertising. If you have the knowhow and you are truly comfortable in front of the camera perhaps you will wish to deliver your own message. If not, delegate that responsibility to someone who will be able to make a good impression for you. Some very unfortunate results can occur when an inexperienced business owner branches into television production and acting. One very effective type of television advertising is a film of work in progress (naturally the groomer will be putting the finishing touches on a *very* cooperative dog) with just a voice-over and perhaps a backup of printed name, telephone number and business hours appearing at the end.

Radio is considerably less expensive than television advertising. In radio the entire effect must be achieved verbally without the added advantage of the visual impression. Skillfully done, this can be a very persuasive form of advertising, and at the beginning of your business venture may prove more economically feasible than television. The same caution about your own "starring role" is also applicable to radio advertising. Before you decide to read your own radio commercial, please take the time to record your own voice on a home tape recorder. You may be surprised. Frequently people simply do not recognize their own voices on a recording and while the radio station will certainly have far more sophisticated equipment than you are likely to have at home, do not expect miracles. The radio stations, like the television stations, have people on staff to read those commercials in a voice that has been carefully trained to project exactly the right image.

Whether you are dealing with television or with radio advertising, work toward a complete message. Be sure that all information is conveyed as clearly and as accurately as possible. Remember that the professionals at the station probably have very little idea just what it is that you do. Although the ad writers will not deliberately mislead the public, you will have the ultimate responsibility for the advertising. This is especially important if your advertising will include some special offer or a new promotion. Be sure that there is virtually no way in which that ad can be construed to mean something you did not intend. A good example might be the announcement that "Dogs will receive a free dip with bath." What you *meant* to say was that dogs would be given a free dip when they had a bath at the regular price. Unfortunately it would be all too easy for the listening public to assume that dogs (maybe all dogs who came in?) would be given a bath and a dip at no charge. No matter how careful you may be, some people will misunderstand your advertising. Try to be as clear as possible. If the radio or television station is doing all the scripts for your advertising, be very sure that you proofread that script before the first time it is aired. Also, be sure to watch or listen to the first air time for your advertising (not that you would miss that for the world) so that any error or confusion can be remedied right away. Many times you will not be charged for the spot in question if the error was on the part of the production staff. Try to develop a good working relationship with these production people. They can really be of enormous service to you and they will be more anxious to do a good job for you if you get along well with them.

The major problem with either television or radio advertising is the fact that it is quite fleeting in nature and unless you are able to afford to keep those spots running consistently you may lose some of the benefits of the wide coverage. Listeners or viewers will possibly remember having heard *something,* but may not be able to recall quite what it was they saw or heard and worse yet, they may not remember the name of your establishment.

There are several other forms of paid publicity. One that can be very cost effective is the use of business cards. These need not be ruinously expensive. There is no need to go for top-of-the-line engraved cards, but do take time to put some thought into the design of your business cards. One thing that will make your card stand out from others is having it printed on colored stock. Light green or pink can be very attractive and also easy to read. Generally speaking, a pastel background with a dark lettering is best. Dark colors with light printing don't seem to have quite the readability of dark print on light cards.

When you were planning your business name, did you also design (or have designed for you) a business logo? If your logo is well designed, attractive and worthy of comment, people will tend to keep your business card for a longer period of time and will be more inclined to show it to friends. Remember that a logo can be much easier to recall than a name.

Here is a helpful hint. Have your printer make up a few copies of your business card in plain black and white for you to put away in your files. The next time you want to use your business logo or lettering for advertising, the black and white copies will print up better than some of the colors you might be using on your cards. Colored ink or paper makes your card more attractive, but these same pretty colors may be difficult to photocopy back into black and white for use in a newspaper ad or for a printed flyer. You may also wish to have a few plain black-and-white copies made of just the logo. It is much easier to have these reduced in size and still maintain good detail. You will be glad that you have these in your files.

When designing your business cards, try to keep them informative without being cluttered. No one is going to read through an encyclopedia of information printed on one tiny little card. The basics of good advertising will apply here—Who, What, When, Where, Why. Who: Your business name. What: Services offered (all breed grooming, specializing in Poodles, terriers only or whatever applies to your shop). When: A brief listing of your hours (such as 8:30-5:30, Tuesday through Saturday). Where: Your address and phone number. Why: If you have chosen a motto as well as a logo this is the place to put it. "Excellence and Economy," "We Strive for Perfection," "Treat your Dog like a Prince," "Pamper your Pet," "A

Four examples of clever and memorable business cards.

Clean Dog is a Healthy Dog," "Be Proud of your Pup." Any of these might make a good short motto. Sometimes a motto is a part of a logo and sometimes it is separate. If your name is well known in the area, be sure to list it on your card as owner. If you are willing to accept after-hours calls at your home, you might list your home phone as well as your business listing. If you don't want to receive calls at all hours of the day and night, then for goodness sake don't put your home number on your business card.

Business cards can be used in a number of ways. Naturally you will always carry your cards with you, and in the event that you are talking to someone (about almost anything, it doesn't have to be about dog grooming), by all means offer them your card. This after all is where you can be reached during the usual business day. If you are ordering new tires for your car it is perfectly reasonable to give the man at the tire store your card. Who knows, he might have a dog, and he certainly has other customers who have dogs.

Another good place to leave your business cards is in pet stores (if the store offers grooming services they probably won't allow you to leave a supply of cards), and certainly in every veterinary clinic in the area that does not have a groomer of its own. In regard to veterinary clinics, this is certainly one area in which good business relations will pay off handsomely. If you are on excellent terms with a veterinarian or two you can reap a handsome dividend in referrals. Sometimes you can also place a few of your business cards near the cash register in a restaurant or other small business. This is especially true if it is a business you patronize frequently. Be alert! Anywhere that you see the business cards of other businesses on display is a prospective place for some cards of your own.

Other forms of printed matter to publicize your business are posters or handbills. These may be small or large, simple or elaborate. Posters are generally a good bit more expensive than flyers or handbills because of the heavy stock on which they are printed. You can cut down on this cost by mounting some of your lighter-weight printed material on colored poster board for a more lasting display. Handbills in a standard 8½-by-11-inch size can be quite adequate. Keeping in mind the same logo or motto you have been using all along as well as the color scheme you have been using on your cards, you should be able to formulate some good ideas for an eye-catching flyer or handbill.

Once you have started to get some ideas about what you want, consult with a printer about costs and the various services available. There are increasing numbers of quick-print shops that do nice work at a very reasonable price. In most cases, the least expensive way to go is for you to do all your own art work and to present this in a finished form to the printer who then simply makes copies of what you have done. The result can range from excellent to awful depending on your own talent. If you are not especially gifted in this field of expertise, it will be to your advantage to seek professional help. The printer will almost certainly be able to give you the help you need, but the cost can mount alarmingly. If you live in an area where there is a college, then by all means contact the art department there. This type of layout is often a specialty of the commercial art program and you may well be able to find a student who will do some exceptional work at a most modest fee. Students need to practice their craft and will be delighted to be able to earn some money doing so. Generally speaking, you will find that a student artist will be inclined to devote more time to your project than an already established artist who is employed in the art field. If you are unable to locate a student artist, how about one of your friends? Don't hesitate to mention what you are working on. You may be pleasantly surprised to find out what talents your friends have that they will be happy to share with you. In this way you should be able to keep printing costs well within your budget. Keep in mind that it will be better for you to spend a little more for a professional-looking flyer than to skimp and look like a real amateur. Never forget that the public will judge you and your ability by the way your advertising looks.

When you are planning your flyers, keep space requirements in mind. The 8½-by-11-inch format is large enough to be effective without being so large as to present problems in finding a place to display it. Veterinarians will often allow you to place one of your flyers on a bulletin board in their clinic if the flyer is not so large that it takes up the entire board. Laundromats frequently have some sort of display area available for their customers. Some grocery stores will allow you to post a flyer in a window. Don't be afraid to ask, but always be sure that you do ask. It is a breach of good manners and possibly of some city ordinances to go around slapping your advertising up without prior permission.

Flyers are sometimes called handbills because they can be used just as the name implies—to hand out. You can do this personally if you have the time and the inclination, or you can hire someone to do it for you. Sometimes a Scout group or other youth organization will take on this sort of job in return for a donation to the organization. The advantage is that you can have a number of people handing out your advertising and covering a wider area in little time. If you choose to do the handing out yourself, you might wish to use a bit of showmanship in your method of distribution. Dress nicely, and take an exquisitely groomed dog with you on a leash. Be sure that you have made an inquiry previously to be sure that you will not be violating any city ordinances in passing out your material. Also be sure that the dog you choose to take with you is one that is glad to meet strangers and is well behaved and gentle. Nothing is more appealing to the public than a really cute dog.

Coupons are another form of advertising that can be of great benefit to the newly established grooming salon. Something free is always an attraction for the public. A discount on popular services is also a good way to tempt folks to try your services. You will be relying on the excellence of your work to bring them back a second time but it is that first visit that is the most difficult to get. Coupons can be incorporated as part of the flyers or handbills you pass out to the public. They can also be left with local veterinarians, kennels or other businesses that might be willing to give them to their customers. If you do choose to use a coupon in conjunction with any of your advertising, be sure that you make the coupon very specific in what is offered. Also be sure that the coupon has a definite expiration date clearly printed on it. You will avoid many unhappy customers if you do this.

Classified newspaper advertising is one of the most cost-efficient forms of advertising available to you. Initially, you may wish to simply insert a small classified ad in the Pets section in your local newpapers or in the Pet Services section if you are advertising in a very large newspaper. One very good way to determine just how much effect your newspaper ad is having is to have some sort of price reduction or special offer for those who present the ad at the time they bring their pet in for grooming. Often a simple "$1.00 off with this ad" line will be enough to let you know just how many people your ad is reaching. Newspaper advertising has the advantage of being somewhat more durable than a radio or television spot in that the customer can at least refer back to the ad or clip it out for future reference. With respect to durability, newspaper advertising is similar to Yellow Pages advertising. Newspapers have one feature that Yellow Pages don't have, and that is that your ad can be changed as often as you like to reflect your latest special or to allow you to experiment wth different wording to see what works best for your specific area.

As your business grows, you may wish to expand your newspaper advertising to match your growing income. The next step in newspaper advertising is to make your classified ad more noticeable by increasing its size. You need not necessarily increase the number of words in the ad itself. The increased white space around your copy will enhance the visibility of the ad greatly. Another way to make your classified ad stand out is to use a heading in a larger type than the type used for the body of the ad.

The next improvement in your newspaper advertising could be to change from classified (or use in addition to your classified ad) to a small display ad. Here you can expect the staff of the newspaper to be of great help to you. Don't hesitate to ask for help in design and composition to produce an appealing and eye-catching advertisement. When planning for display advertising, be sure you have some idea where this ad will appear within the newspaper. One nice place to specify, if you are given a choice, is the Sunday TV section if your newspaper has one. The benefit here is obvious. The TV section from the Sunday newspaper is the one section most subscribers or even casual purchasers will keep for the entire week. Thus your display ad is kept in their homes all week long and has that much better a chance to be seen. Ideally, you would wish to have your ad appear in the first couple of pages in the TV section. That way readers won't overlook it until the last day or two of the week.

Paid advertising, like so many other aspects of opening a new business, can cost a modest sum or it can cost a phenomenal amount. You must be the judge. Foremost in your mind must be your budget. By all means use paid advertising. Use it right up to your budgeted amount, but don't let advertising eat up so much of your working capital that you find yourself in a financial bind.

FREE ADVERTISING

Advertising in an absolute necessity for any new business. Keep firmly in mind, however, that advertising doesn't always mean *paid* advertising. Some of the most effective advertising you can ever have is absolutely free.

One of the most beneficial forms of advertising for any business is just plain word of mouth. Nothing will reflect on you quite so favorably as the praise of a satisfied customer. You are certainly aware that pet owners take their pets very seriously and they can be most appreciative of good service (they can also do you great harm if your service is shabby) and will be more than glad to recommend you to their friends and acquaintances. You might be surprised to find how well and how far word of mouth will spread. A satisfied owner might be sitting in the veterinary clinic waiting for his dog's annual check up and he may strike up a conversation with another dog owner. You can bet that your satisfied client will tell all about you and your wonderful shop and your marvelous service. This form of advertising is unbelievably valuable. Honest praise coming from someone who has availed himself of your services will be more believable to the hearer than any other form of advertising. The line of reasoning seems to be simply that this client has no personal interest in your business and must have been very happy with your work to recommend it to others. Some extremely successful businesses have made their entire way with nothing but word-of-mouth advertising.

The best possible way to encourage this type of advertising is to be especially accommodating to your customers. If you genuinely care about your customers and their dogs, you will soon find that your customers genuinely care about you. They will soon sense your sincerity. By the same token, if you are not sincere in your wish to serve your clients they will sense that fact also, no matter how outwardly pleasant you may be.

Extra favors are always a delight to the recipient. It will help your business if you are sure to let the client know tactfully that you are doing a special favor. Perhaps you might say something like, "We don't usually stay open late on Tuesdays, but Spot is one of our favorites, so just for you we'll let you come in fifteen minutes after our regular closing time, just this one time." This lets the client know that you are giving him a special service, and it also lets him know, tactfully, that he shouldn't expect to make this a regular habit. You can add extra emphasis to this kind of remark by saying to the client, "Please don't tell anyone we did this for you because we don't stay late as a rule." In this way you make the client feel even more special and, if you are lucky, the client really won't tell anyone else that you stayed open late (or whatever it was that you did), and the customers this client sends to you will be less likely to expect you to stay late any time they come after hours. Remember that each and every one of us likes to feel special. Anything you do that makes your client feel special or makes him feel that his dog is a special favorite of yours is going to add luster to your reputation. It could be something as small as calling to remind the client of an appointment, or calling between appointments to check on their pet if you discover some problem. Any little thing you do for that client will come back to you greatly increased and your reputation and your clientele will grow.

Another form of unpaid advertising is the press release. If you have some talent with the written word, it will be quite possible for you to write your own press release and simply mail copies to every newspaper in your area. This sort of material should always be written in the third person. The heading might simply read something like, "New Dog Salon in Area," or "Dogs Need Good Grooming Too," or "For the Pet Who has Everything" or "Area Dogs now Have own Beauty Shop." Try to remember while you are composing your press release that you are going to be sending this information to a newspaper. Because the primary function of the newspaper is news, you must make your press release read like news rather than like an advertisement. Be sure to list your own credentials just as if it had been a reporter writing the article. By all means, list your membership in various civic or professional organizations together with any offices you might have held in those organizations. Your hobbies are also a part of your press release. Yours might read something like this: "Mrs. X's hobbies include growing prize-winning roses as well as prize-winning dogs. She has exhibited both and has many trophies and ribbons garnered by her winners." It is also perfectly permissible to include a direct quotation from the person about whom the press release has been written. A nice informal quotation might go something like this: "Drop in and see our new shop. We are always glad to meet new folks and have a chance to talk dogs with them. Rose growers are welcome too." Try to get in lots of detail without making the entire press release sound like an advertisement.

Another excellent way to get your name before the pet-owning public is to do something newsworthy. No, don't rob the local bank—keep your newsworthy activities on a very positive note. How about volunteering to groom one dog each week for the local humane organization at no charge? The stated objective of course is

94

to help the dog have a more appealing look for prospective adopters (and it does help), but you will also benefit by keeping your name and your work before the public. If your humane shelter has a "pet of the week" photo in the newspaper, be sure to ask someone from the shelter to bring the dog into your shop for its grooming session and then have the newspaper photographer take its picture there. You can almost guarantee a nice little mention in the newpaper (This week's pet was groomed by so-and-so of so-and-so's grooming shop.) and with just a little luck you may be able to end up with a full-scale interview. By all means, tell the newspaper folks that you will be happy to do a step-by-step grooming for the photographer. If you are taken up on this offer, be sure to explain to the photographer just how the photos should be planned because he probably does not have much experience with dog grooming. You will also want to let the photographer know that it might take a fair amount of time for him to complete the series of photos. You might even wish to sit down and write out a list of the steps to be included. Naturally, the photographer and ultimately the editor will be the ones to choose which pictures will appear, but at least be sure no pictures are going to be used that could be misinterpreted as some sort of unkindness. The only exception to this rule is the miserable-dog-in-bathtub shot, which seems so dear to the hearts of newspaper photographers. When planning this photo session, be sure to make plans to have on hand a dog who is not only cute but very *very* cooperative. This will make it much easier on everyone concerned and will lessen the chance of having less-than-flattering pictures appear in the newspaper.

Almost any sort of newsworthy event can be brought to the attention of the press and can result in the mention of your name and often the name of your business. If one of your own dogs is a winner at a dog show or obedience trial, be sure to let your local newspaper know. If you have guests in from out of town, be sure that it is mentioned in the appropriate column in the newspaper (this is especially applicable if you live in a small town). If you are elected to a post in some organization, be sure that the newspaper is given a list of all the new officers. In short, keep your name before the public.

TRUTH IN ADVERTISING

One word of warning is appropriate in this discussion of advertising. By all means, tell the whole world what you can do, but please don't claim to be able to do things you cannot do. It is far better to be a bit modest in your claims and to let your very satisfied clientele do the boasting for you than to fall short of the claims you might have made. If you are capable of preparing a particular breed for the show ring, then by all means do advertise the fact, but don't claim to be able to do all breeds for the show ring unless that is truly the case.

TIMING AND BUDGET

Timing will be important in your first advertising campaign. Unless you plan to sit idle for the first few days after your initial opening, it would be wise to plan for some advertising to appear prior to the time you expect to open your doors. This advertising should be designed to whet the interest of the public and get you started. If you plan a grand opening, by all means begin early to announce the date and the planned activities. That might be a good time to arrange tours or an open house of your new grooming salon. If you have been grooming in another location or have been working at home, be sure to send invitations to your clients. This is a good time for an open house because you can have everything sparkling clean and very neat and well organized. If you plan to have any work going on during an open house, be sure that the dogs on display are very cooperative and seem to be happy about being groomed. This makes a nice impression.

It is to be hoped that you have planned your advertising budget for the entire year. In allocating the amount of money you will be spending at any given time, you may wish to distribute that budgeted amount in such a way that you allow yourself extra funds for your first advertising campaign and perhaps for one or two special campaigns during the balance of the year. Otherwise, simply plan to spend a certain amount each month and stick to that amount. Don't let salesmen talk you into advertising you cannot afford.

Don't be discouraged if the first few days or even weeks don't bring a flood of clients to your door. Remember that the work you do will sell itself and the first few clients will gradually bring in others, and before you know it you will have more work to do than you can handle. Just let your business grow stronger and stronger as time goes on. Set your goals and work toward those goals. Keep in mind that dog grooming is a service business and that *caring* service is the key to your success.

96

7

Just Ask the Groomer . . .

The Questions are Inevitable

T HE DAY YOU open your grooming salon doors to the public is the day you become, like it or not, an expert on the widest possible range of subjects. In fact, you will be considered an expert on everything pertaining to dogs. This is a strange phenomenon. It is amazing to contemplate, but many of your clients will seek your advice (and will take that advice) in preference to the advice of a veterinarian or dog-training expert who might be far better qualified to answer the question. Occasionally (or maybe more than occasionally), medical questions are posed to the groomer in the hope that the client will thus be able to save a trip to the veterinary clinic and the cost of that visit. More often however, you will be asked questions simply because your clients make the assumption that, because you are in a business dealing with dogs, you know all there is to be known about dogs, including their behavior, diseases, training, care, reproduction and anything else you might think of, as well as some things you might not think of. In fact, some of your clients will make that leap in logic a bit longer and will presume that you also will have the same information about other animals of all sorts as well.

You will probably be asked some questions that will seem almost unbelievable. In general, the public is not at all well informed about dogs. You will find that many of your clients still believe in some of the most preposterous old wives' tales imaginable. In some cases, this makes no difference to you in your work and you can simply ignore these beliefs. Other things you may have to try to explain. Sometimes you will be successful in making the client understand the realities of the situation and sometimes you will not. One commonly held belief that might affect you is the belief that an Old English Sheepdog will go blind if the hair is cut away from his face so that his eyes are left without a screen of hair. Of course this is not true and when faced with a severely matted and dirty Old English Sheepdog it will be important for you to gently make the client understand that having all that mess cut away from the dog's face is, in fact, of real benefit to the dog.

Some owners will tell you in absolute seriousness that their dog is embarrassed by being trimmed too short and will hide away. This is not necessarily going to be a problem to you unless the dog is so terribly matted that he must be clipped very short. Then your job becomes that of advocate for the dog. Agreeing with the client helps. You will be amazed at how quickly you can get an owner to see your point of view if you remember to begin your remarks with "I understand how he must feel." Everyone wants to be understood. You can help to win the client toward your views simply by letting him know that you do understand. Try to understand what the client is really saying. In this case, the client is actually saying that *he* is embarrassed. He feels that you are going to judge him for neglecting his dog so he projects his feeling of embarrassment onto the dog and invents what sounds like a plausible reason for having allowed the dog to reach such a state of mats and tangles.

Another commonly held belief that will affect you is that the very best way to remove tangles from a dog is to give the dog a bath. Of course, you know that the absolute worst thing you can possibly do to a dog with a matted coat is to apply shampoo and water. Some owners honestly misunderstand the so-called "tangle-free" shampoos. They are under the impression that this type of shampoo will actually remove tangles that are already present. Owners will often bring in a dog who is amazingly clean but is matted into a solid mass and will tell you sincerely that they simply can't understand why his coat is such a mess. After all, he is bathed every single week.

Some of the questions you will be asked are straightforward and are ones you will be quite well qualified to answer. These are the questions that are within your special field of expertise. Things like, "What is the best shampoo to use on my dog?"; "How often should my dog have his hair cut to keep him looking nice?"; "What style trim would be most flattering to my dog?"; "What kind of brush or comb is best to use on this kind of coat?"; "Why doesn't my dog look as nice after I give him a bath as he does after you do it?"; "I am afraid to cut my dog's nails, won't he bleed to death?" and many other questions in this same vein.

You are going to be simply amazed at the lack of basic information among your clients. Don't be critical. This lack of information is one of the main reasons you will have a good business. It isn't only that your clients don't have time to maintain their pets (Although this is true in some cases. A few of your customers will know how to care for the dog, but will simply not have the time or the inclination to do it.). In the vast majority of instances, you will find that the owner just plain doesn't have any idea how to keep his dog well groomed, which is exactly why he is willing to pay you for this service.

TEACHING BASIC CARE

It is remarkable how many people will purchase a pup and have no idea what the grooming requirements might be for that particular breed. Even more astounding is that breeders often do not make the buyer aware that the pup will need special grooming (afraid they might lose a sale?) and the poor buyer leaves well enough alone until the day he discovers the pup has somehow gotten in really bad condition. That is when the groomer is called in.

This is an area of disagreement. Some groomers absolutely will not explain maintenance grooming to their clients. They feel this will hurt their business by allowing the owner to bring his dog in less frequently. Not so. In fact, the time that you spend teaching an owner simple brushing technique usually will pay off many times over. In the first place, by answering the owner's questions you have shown yourself to be interested and helpful. Furthermore, even when shown some basic coat care, most of your clients will prefer to let you do the majority of the work, especially when they discover that brushing is more time consuming than it looks. Try always to be generous with your answers to grooming questions. Especially, feel free to show the client the kind of brushes you use, and by all means tell the customer where to buy a good brush so that he will not mess

Hair is clipped close on the head of the Cocker Spaniel. Some pet owners prefer that no topknot be left at all.

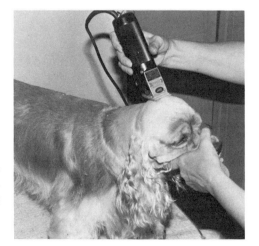

Hold the dog's mouth firmly shut while clipping the chin.

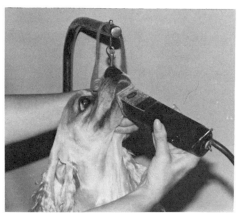

The outside of the ear is clipped against the growth to blend smoothly into the hair on the back of the skull.

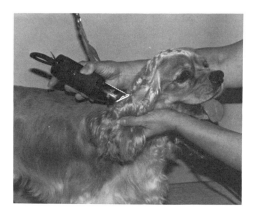

up the dog's coat and skin by using poor-quality equipment. Another benefit is that those customers who do learn good basic care will usually bring their dogs in for regular grooming, and those dogs will be some of the easiest you will do because they are well kept at home.

BEING INFORMED ABOUT THE AKC

Chances are, you are well qualified to answer a variety of questions not strictly in the area of dog grooming. This is especially true if you have been involved for some time in breeding, showing or training your own dogs. You will almost certainly be asked questions about dog registration, litter registrations, transfers of ownership and lost papers. If you are not extremely well informed on these topics, it is easy to become so. Simply write to the American Kennel Club, 51 Madison Avenue, New York, New York 10010, and request a copy of their publication entitled *American Kennel Club Rules for Registration and Dog Shows.* This will be sent to you at no charge and is a wonderful reference for you to keep at hand. The AKC has several other publications you might request also. These include one pertaining to obedience trials and one that deals with registering dogs purchased in foreign countries. Believe it or not, over the course of time you will almost certainly be asked questions about all these topics. It is so easy to have the information and so much better to be well informed than to pass along the wrong information. Remember, it does not reflect well on your expertise to pass on incorrect information even if the information is on a topic that is not really a part of dog grooming as such. The public will tend to believe that if you were incorrect on one subject, you may not know what you are talking about on another topic.

QUESTIONS ABOUT BEHAVIOR

Dog behavior is another topic that will be asked about often. You will get questions about everything from housebreaking the new pup to serious behavior problems. There will be times when you will hardly be able to believe the things some owners will tolerate from their dogs. If you are truly knowledgeable about dog behavior, then perhaps you will want to try to answer questions in this area. If you have had dogs for many years, there is little doubt that you will have your own opinions about most of the questions you will be

Beginning at the occipital point, the coat on the neck is clipped in the direction of growth.

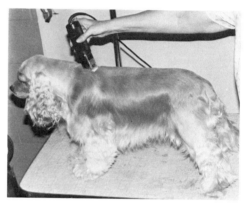

The coat on the back, from the withers to the tip of the tail, is clipped in the direction of growth.

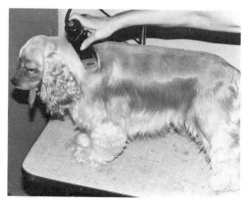

The direction of growth changes on the shoulder, hip and side of the dog and the groomer must change the direction of clipping in order to achieve a smooth result.

asked about dog behavior. Be careful. Remember that the owner considers you the total expert. Some things are far more complicated than they seem on the surface. Some behavior problems need expert analysis by someone with great experience in the field of dog behavior and in the modification of that behavior. Perhaps you are qualified, through your experience and training, to help your clients with this sort of problem. If so, try to answer their questions. If not, say so! Your clients will have far more respect for you if you will say to them "I'm really sorry, I don't know the answer to that question, but perhaps you might call so-and-so." Mention the name of someone you feel might be better qualified to answer the question. Some behavior problems are actually in your field of grooming. One of the most common is, "He just won't let me brush him. What can I do?" Of course you know how to answer that question and by all means you should answer the client to the best of your ability. You must realize, however, that the client may not take your advice.

Some clients seem to think that groomers practice some form of witchcraft to keep dogs quiet while they are being groomed. Other folks are under the impression that all dogs are tranquilized for grooming (a practice that is extremely dangerous) and these people need your reassurance that their dog will neither be drugged nor hexed while at your shop.

QUESTIONS YOU SHOULD NOT ANSWER

Even though you may be extraordinarily well qualified in virtually all phases of dog care, breeding and training, not to mention dog grooming, there is almost certainly one area in which you are not qualified. That area is the field of veterinary medicine. Very few dog groomers are also veterinarians. (To be perfectly fair, the other side of the coin is also true. Very few veterinarians are dog groomers and sometimes they need your advice.) This means you must be very careful about answering medical questions or anything that could possibly be construed as a medical question. Veterinarians can sometimes be extremely touchy if they think someone is handing out medical advice they should be getting paid to dispense. It is to be hoped that you have a good working relationship with one or more veterinarians in your area and that you will be able to quote their opinions for your clientele on some simple questions. Your quotations must be kept to a minimum and must be carefully stated. You should also ask permission to quote your veterinarian.

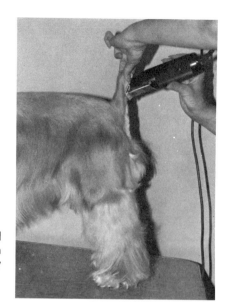

The underside of the tail is NEVER clipped against the direction of growth as shown here. Hair near the anus is carefully trimmed with the grain.

Shears are used to shape the long coat on the leg. Notice that the shears are being used in the same direction that the hair grows. Cutting across the direction of growth will result in unsightly scissor marks.

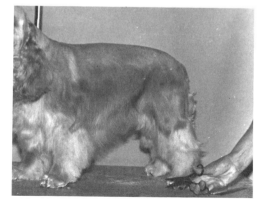

With the dog's foot resting on the table, the hair is scissored neatly around the foot. The shears are held at a ninety-degree angle to the table.

Unfortunately, veterinarians do not seem to have any qualms about handing out grooming advice. You are in a somewhat different position. There really aren't any laws that would prohibit a veterinarian from practicing dog grooming without a license, but most states certainly do have laws pertaining to practicing veterinary medicine without a license. In some cases, simply answering a question is considered to be practicing medicine.

One very real problem area lies within your clients' hearing and comprehension. You may be astounded to hear yourself quoted. Some of the things attributed to you will be so farfetched that they could be included in a "Ripley's Believe It or Not," but unfortunately, that is exactly what the customer thought you said. This is a situation that will sometimes cause conflict between a groomer and a veterinarian. And this is why it is so very necessary for you to have a solid relationship with the local veterinarians. If you are known to be sensible and not prone to giving out medical advice, then the veterinarians will tend to respect you and discount some of the more outrageous things attributed to you. By all means be ready to render this same courtesy to the veterinarian with regard to the things he is quoted as having said about grooming.

REFERRALS

One very important way to build a genuine rapport with local veterinarians and to render good service to your clients at the same time is to refer medical questions to the veterinarian. This is not a brush-off by any means. You will certainly understand how worried the client must be. At the same time, protect yourself by recommending that the client call his veterinarian. This is especially true if the question seems to involve an emergency situation. Here again, you will hardly believe some of the questions you will be asked, like, "My dog was hit by a car. He is unconscious, but he is breathing. What shall I do?" Your answer of course, would be to wrap the dog in a blanket and get him to a doctor immediately. In this type of situation try to avoid any lengthy conversation. You may be surprised that the owner will want to continue to question you. Don't allow this to happen. Time could be critical and this is absolutely a medical question.

Dog groomers are often more familiar with the dogs they groom than the owners are. This is especially true of things such as ear mites or ear infections, anal gland problems, badly-cared-for

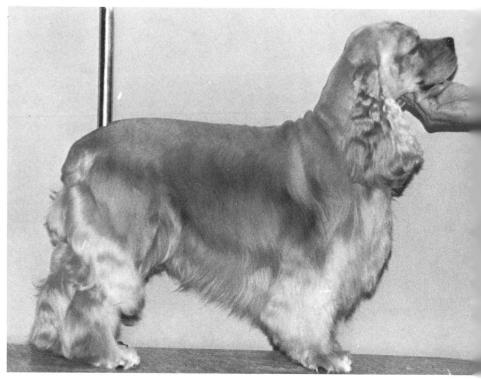

The completed Cocker Spaniel presents a finished appearance. The Cocker Spaniel is one the breeds that most all-breed salons do frequently.

teeth, warts, cysts and skin conditions of all sorts. These are situations that should be called to the owner's attention so that the dog can make a visit to the vet. This is an especially touchy situation with some veterinarians. While they are more than glad to see, diagnose and treat the problem, they don't want you to presume to make any diagnoses. Unless your veterinarian is practically your best friend he will resent it if you send one of your clients to him with a ready-made diagnosis. Every doctor likes to make his own decisions and most take the position that any correct diagnosis made by a nonmedical person was simply a lucky guess. Try to see his side of the matter. If you make a correct diagnosis (or guess) it leaves the impression with the client that the only reason he had to go to that veterinary clinic was to get medication for the problem. This relegates the veterinarian to performing as little more than a pharmacist. The veterinarian *is* a doctor and he did not spend a number of years in medical school to be demoted to pharmacist.

There are many tactful ways to handle the discovery of a medical problem with one of your clients' dogs. If you notice the problem before you accept the dog, by all means bring it to the attention of the owner. Do this in a nonaccusatory way, but bring it to the attention of the owner so that *you* don't get blamed for the problem. Owners will sometimes try to blame you for a problem that was already present. This is especially true with skin problems. The client may be quick to claim that you have "clipper burned" his dog, when in fact the animal has inflicted all the irritation upon himself scratching fleas. Unfortunately, some veterinarians will also make this kind of snap diagnosis.

As you are accepting the dog for grooming, a quick check will often reveal some of these problems. Then you might say, "Oh my! He has really chewed at this leg hasn't he?" Or "Poor little guy has been scratching at his ears." This gives you the opportunity to volunteer to check his ears and see if there is a problem. You were going to do that anyway, but now you are able to make a special point of it and it then assumes the status of doing the client a real favor. If the ears do look bad, an appropriate way to handle the situation is simply to tell the owner that "We cleaned a lot of dark tarry material out of his ears, and they certainly do look a bit swollen. You really should take him to see the vet before they get any worse." Now is when you will be asked, "What do you think is wrong with his ears?" Even though you feel sure that you know what is wrong with his ears, your best answer is going to be along these lines: "Well, in order to really know what is wrong, you have to be able to see into the ear itself. I can't honestly say what's wrong, but I would certainly have it looked at." In this way, you have made no diagnosis to offend the doctor, you have done the dog the favor of sending him for medical treatment and you have made the client feel that you are truly concerned for his dog's welfare. You may wish to send a note with the client to the doctor telling him how the ear looked before cleaning and the color of the matter removed. In this note you should also mention how the ear was cleaned, whether with dry cotton, alcohol, peroxide or baby oil. Even if you don't send a note, the veterinarian will almost certainly be told that you sent the dog to be seen. The owner will report that you cleaned "black stuff" out of the dog's ears and the doctor will begin to respect you for being able to recognize a situation that required medical intervention.

Teeth are another area that will necessitate referrals to the veterinarian. It is not at all uncommon to have the owner complain of his dog's foul breath. The very first thing to check is the teeth. If it is an old dog or one of the toy breeds, you will often find the teeth crusted with tartar. By all means send the dog to the doctor for dental care. Bad teeth can give rise to a wide variety of other ills. Teeth (or ears) that are in bad condition can also cause the entire dog to have a bad odor. The client will be grateful that his dog no longer smells bad and you will get the credit. You knew just what to look for and were able to recommend just the right thing to do about it. You may also have to remind your clients from time to time that their dogs' teeth should be cleaned. Often the owner who wouldn't dream of neglecting anything else has never even looked inside his dog's mouth.

Skin problems are frequently first noticed by the groomer. Again, this should mean a trip to the vet's office. Skin conditions are so varied that they can sometimes be difficult even for the veterinarian to diagnose, so don't you try. If you discover lumps, lesions, warts, moles, areas that appear swollen or reddened, be sure to point these out to the owner when the dog is picked up, and make the recommendation for a visit to the veterinary clinic. You may in time view some pretty shocking things hidden under a matted coat. It is unbelievable what an owner will miss entirely.

If, during the time a dog is being groomed, you discover a condition that appears to be serious, it is wise to call the owner immediately, ask if he is aware of this situation and make the recommendation that the dog be taken to the doctor as soon as he is finished with his grooming. This allows the owner time to call the clinic for an appointment. Naturally, if the problem is an emergency, ask the owner to pick the dog up right away and take it to the veterinary clinic.

Don't be surprised if you are asked to perform a variety of medical services. You may be asked to give immunizations, dock puppy tails, crop ears or even to do a spay surgery. The public seems unable to sort out the difference between veterinarians and groomers. Always keep in mind that you are not a doctor and could be prosecuted for performing any sort of treatment for the public. In some cases, the line between your job and that of the veterinarian will be a fine one. This is especially true of things like ear cleaning and emptying the anal glands. Use your common sense and you will not be likely to have a problem.

As a professional groomer, you can be the first line of defense for the health of the dogs you groom. You are far more aware and far more knowledgeable than the vast majority of the owners who will be bringing their dogs to you for grooming. You are in a position to check over virtually every square inch of the dog as he is being groomed. You can do a good turn for the dog and for his owner by catching problems before they become serious. Your expertise will make you more aware of things that are not as they should be. At the same time you are doing yourself and your business a good turn by making your client feel special and cared for.

Knowing what questions you can answer and what questions you should refer to the veterinarian or another specialist is very important. Only you can assess your capabilities and range of knowledge. Try to look at your own abilities objectively and don't be afraid to say "I really don't know."

One thing to remember is that you are in the business of dog grooming, not the business of answering questions. If you are not careful, you may find yourself using a vast amount of time answering a multitude of questions. If you have the time and the inclination to answer these questions, fine. Just don't let your business suffer because you are allowing callers to keep you tied up with questions. If you are busy, offer to call back or ask the caller to call at a more convenient time.

Above all, when asked the million-and-one questions you are

sure to be asked, try not to make any caller feel that his question is stupid. Every caller is a potential client and the only stupid question is the question that remains unasked.

8

You Want It Done When? . . .

Scheduling Your Time

IF YOU PLAN to be a successful businessperson, scheduling your time is going to play an important part in your life. Because you are going into business for yourself, you will be the one who will plan your schedule, revise the schedule if necessary and take charge of your own time. The key is just that: Taking charge of your time. Drifting through your days with no idea what comes next is not the most direct route to success. In fact, few people just drift into success at all. No matter whether your goal is simply to have a modest business that will produce a comfortable income, or to become a self-made big-time businessperson, you must know where you are going, set your goals and make your plans to get there. In setting those goals, be realistic. In order to reach a goal, you must view that goal as being within your reach. First set an overall goal, then break that goal into the steps that will take you to the place you wish to be. Now, make each of those steps a goal within itself. Never forget that you are in charge and you can revise your goals as well as your time schedule. You never fail—you simply revise your goals.

USING YOUR APPOINTMENT BOOK

Your appointment book is, or should be, one of the most important business tools you will ever have. Your entire business will eventually center around the appointment book and the schedule you have arranged within it.

The actual format of your appointment book will depend on what you want and need. This is a very individual sort of thing and there are many ways to set this up. There are all sorts of appointment books available. They may be found in your local office-supply store, drug store, department store or beauty-supply store. In fact, the office-supply store and the beauty-supply store are the two places most likely to have an appointment book that will best fill your needs. Take the time to look around before you make a purchase. Keep in mind your own schedule and then look at the appointment books that are available to you.

The calendar-type appointment book is not usually satisfactory because there is simply not enough writing space allotted to each day within it. This type of calendar shows a full month, and consequently, each day is shown as a square of approximately 1½ to 2 inches. This will not really allow you enough space for the information you will want to record.

The book-type appointment calendar is usually more suitable to the sort of schedule you will want to keep. One of the ones on the market is called "Week-at-a-Glance." This particular format allows two pages for each full week. There are three vertical columns on each page, and Saturday and Sunday are in the same column on the right-hand side of the right-hand page. The one disadvantage with this particular book is the fact that Saturday is not allotted as much space as the rest of the days, and if you plan to work all day on Saturday (or Sunday for that matter), this is a little confining. It is not, however, a serious problem. If you need more space, the same company also manufactures a similar book called "Day-at-a-Glance," which allots an entire page to each day. These are usually available at office-supply stores.

The appointment books designed specifically for beauticians are quite suitable for the sort of work you will be doing. These are usually available at an office-supply store or at a beauty-supply store.

You may want to experiment a bit before you find the format most comfortable for you, but once you have set up a format you like, stick with it. Having a basic format makes it easy for you to look at your calendar and know quickly what is going on.

There are several things you will need to know about each dog scheduled to come in for grooming. You will of course be keeping a card file on your various clients, but you will need to have certain basic information to help you with your scheduling and you will not want to have to refer to the file repeatedly, so this information must be shown in your appointment book.

The basic information you will need to have at your fingertips when booking appointments will be fairly simple: Time—you will have the time at which you are expecting this dog to come in; Name—the dog's name and the owner's name. In a busy shop, the simple notation "Fluffy" might be any one of several dogs of several different breeds. One way to indicate which animal you are dealing with is to list the dog's name and the owner's last name. Thus, Fluffy becomes "Fluffy Smith." This will allow you to find Fluffy's card easily when the day arrives for him or her to be groomed. Unless Fluffy Smith has been in for grooming on such a regular basis that you know what kind of dog he is, you will also want to note the breed. If this is a new client, you may wish to note "new" next to the name and list the phone number. It is not necessary to list a phone number for dogs that have already been in once because this information is listed on the file card. If there is a special rush for this particular dog to be completed, do list the fact because this will affect the scheduling for the day.

The appointment book is not the place to list special requests, styling or other informational notes. These things should be listed on the card or on a special grooming slip when the dog is actually brought in for grooming. The exceptions to this might be the dog coming in for toenail trimming only, or for a bath only instead of a full grooming. A notation to that effect will let you know that you need not plan to spend as much time with this particular dog as you would have to spend if it were coming in for a complete grooming. On the other hand, if the owner tells you that the dog is in really bad condition and has a lot of tangles and mats, you will want to make a brief note to remind you that you will probably need to spend more than the usual amount of time with this dog.

It is important to you to have a rough idea about the various dogs that will be coming in on a given day for several reasons. You will know how many dogs you will be able to schedule for that day, and you will also be able to tell the owners what time to expect their dogs to be ready to go home. It is very irritating to the dog owner to show up at the time he was told the dog would be ready only to be told to come back in an hour or so. Respect the client's time just as much as you expect the client to respect yours.

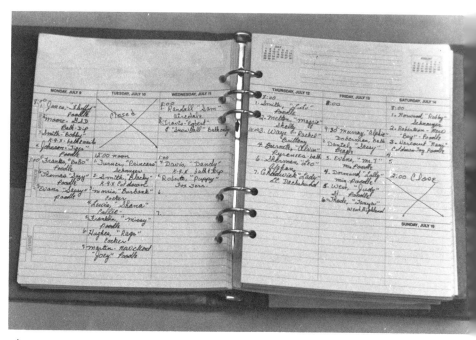

This appointment book allows the groomer to see quickly what the schedule is for the entire week. Those times when the shop is closed have been crossed out in advance to avoid mistakes in scheduling appointments.

Standing Appointments

The backbone of any grooming business is the repeat visit. The more of your clientele who have standing appointments, the better off you will be as a groomer. In some of the most elite shops, prospective clients must go on a waiting list in order to obtain one of the coveted standing appointments. Failure to keep a standing appointment without notifying the shop can result in losing that spot. You will probably not be in a position to make this sort of rule right at first, but you will want to aim for that enviable situation. Encourage your clients to make a repeat appointment at the time they pick up their dog. A good moment to make this suggestion is when the client is making complimentary remarks about the way the dog looks. One way to lead into this is to agree that "Yes, he really does look nice doesn't he? Shall we set up his next appointment for four or six weeks from now, so that he will stay in good shape all the time?" Have that appointment book open and ready. Chances are the client will say "Oh, how about six weeks?" Your reply, "Great! Would Tuesday or Wednesday be better for you?" Always give the client a choice of days. When the client has chosen a day of the week, you can say something to the effect of "O.K., that's six weeks from tomorrow, Tuesday at 9:00 A.M. I'll be sure to call and remind you of the appointment."

Holiday Bookings

If a holiday season is approaching, try to be sure to remind your clients that you will be especially busy at that time and that they will need to get their regular appointments into your book early to assure that they will have their choice of times. An example of this kind of scheduling is to start with your regular clients in October and schedule a November grooming appointment and a Christmas appointment. In this way, you won't find yourself in the awkward position of having to deny an appointment to someone who has been a regular client all year. Your clients like to feel they are special and this is one way to give them that feeling. You might even say something like, "We want to be sure that our regulars have first choice of those Christmas appointments. You know, some people only have their dog done during the holiday season and it's only fair to be sure that the once-a-year people don't crowd out our year-round clients." This is the absolute truth. It really isn't fair to your faithful, year-round clients to deny them an appointment in favor of someone who only shows up during the two weeks prior to the holiday season. Remember that those standing appointments are your bread and butter. They are the people who pay the rent and the utilities and your salary, and best of all, they are the folks who build your business by recommending your work to their friends.

None of this is meant to imply that you should ignore or turn away the people who first call you for an appointment during a holiday season. This is a wonderful time to build your clientele and to develop more regular customers. Every new client is of course a potential standing appointment. Recognize that the holiday season is the busiest season of the year for a grooming business. Don't expect to be able to take your vacation during a major holiday season if you are trying to build a substantial business. There are plenty of other times during the year for you to take your vacations, and you must set your priorities. It is important to have vacation time, but it is also important to build your business.

ASKING FOR REPEAT BUSINESS

Standing appointments will eventually build your business to the level at which you wish to keep it. Because this is the case, it is important that you learn to ask for that repeat business. Often your client will not really think of rescheduling at the time he picks his dog up. The client will think of a grooming appointment when the dog begins to look or smell as if he needs to go to the groomer. You are the one who must plant the suggestion in his mind. You are also the one who is going to have to remind the client that it is time for the dog to have another grooming. Some of your clients will be on a four-week or five-week schedule, probably the most frequently chosen interval is six weeks. Some will be on an eight-week appointment schedule and a few will want to have the dog done only every twelve weeks.

You must respect the client's wishes. Perhaps the client genuinely cannot afford to have his dog groomed more often than every twelve weeks. If the long interval between groomings is causing a grooming problem, such as severe matting, which is increasing the cost of grooming, point out to the client that he could have the dog done more often for very little more money because there would not be additional charges for mats and tangles. In some cases, the owner doesn't care for the freshly clipped look. In that instance, perhaps you could suggest that the dog be left a bit more natural in appearance and groomed a little more frequently.

Many owners have no idea what their dog needs in the way of grooming. Often new owners are not even aware that the breed they have chosen is going to require any particular sort of grooming in order to look like a member of his breed. In rare instances, you may even encounter the uninformed individual who thinks that his Poodle puppy will simply grow into some sort of pattern. These owners are generally appalled to discover that the only way to keep their pet looking like a Poodle is through regular grooming. Some of these owners will develop into good standing-appointment-type clients, some will not.

In asking for repeat business, do not discount the owners of the wonderful mixed-breed dogs who come through your doors. Most established salons have a sizable clientele among the group of dogs frequently called "just plain mutts." Even the owners of these dogs will often be heard to describe their pets in that way, but don't be fooled. These dogs are just as much candidates for the standing-appointment list as any purebred show dog. In fact, the percentage of actual show dogs who will come in for grooming is likely to be quite small.. Most show-dog owners learn to groom their own dogs, and do quite a nice job of it. The only groomer who is likely to have a number of show dogs among the regular clientele will be the groomer who makes a specialty of show-grooming one or more particular breeds.

Reminders

In working with your standing appointments, it is important to keep several things in mind. The first thing to remember is that your client will most likely not remember the dog's grooming appointment without some help from you. This can take the form of a reminder card and/or a telephone call. Another fact you must recognize is that sometimes a standing appointment must be changed to another day. This change can be for many reasons, but it will happen from time to time. Some shops have a hard-and-fast rule that changes must be made twenty-four hours in advance. This is a difficult rule to enforce. Sometimes the owner himself doesn't know until the last minute that a change must be made. It is most important for you to be understanding of the needs of your clients. A dog-grooming salon is a *service* business.

Although you must respect your clients' needs and wishes, it is also important that they understand that this is your business, not your hobby. There are ways to impress that fact on the client without becoming argumentative about it. In fact, you can make the client aware that this is a business and that you are in fact a very busy person and still seem to bend over backward to make the accommodation to the client. The first time a client rearranges a standing appointment should probably not call for any particular action, and if this is a regular client of long standing who has to rearrange suddenly, you will certainly be as helpful as possible. On the other hand, standing appointment does mean *standing* appointment and if the client is in the habit of postponing or rearranging the dog's appointment week after week, or if every time the dog is scheduled to come the owner must make other plans, then sometimes it will be important to explain that you are very busy and that you are making an appointment so that the client's dog can be sure of having time set aside for him. You might make those rearrangements a bit harder to come by. Perhaps you could say something like "Move him to next Monday? Oh, Mrs. Jones, I am so sorry. I don't have a thing available until Thursday next week. Would Thursday morning be O.K.?" Don't panic if Mrs. Jones says no. She will probably try to get someone who will do her dog at a moment's notice. She will soon find that this is easier said than done. If clients are pleased with your work, you will find they will learn to respect standing appointments and to keep them. As time goes on, you will also discover that your regular customers will call you well in advance if it becomes necessary to change an appointment date.

One way for you to handle your reminders is simply to set aside some time at the end of each day to call and remind every appointment for the following day. By doing this you will know whether you have any openings for the next day and you will be able to handle last-minute calls.

LAST MINUTE CALLS

One thing every grooming salon must deal with is the last-minute call. These can take a couple different forms. One of course is the regular client who needs to have his dog done for some special reason. Naturally, you will wish to make every effort to accommodate that need. Sometimes this will mean rearranging your schedule or even staying a little late, but the good will you will earn will more than repay the inconvenience. Once in a while a regular client's dog will suffer some sort of mishap that will require immediate attention from the groomer, and again you will want to make every effort to help with the problem.

The other type of last-minute call is from someone who is new and has never been to your shop before. Or it may be from someone who has had a dog groomed at your shop in the distant past. In the case of the caller who is a totally new client, a fair policy to follow is to do the dog if you are able to do so without disrupting your regular schedule. Let the caller know that you normally expect to have advance notice, but that you will be able to fit his dog into your schedule. You may even wish to say something like "You are really in luck, I just had a call from a regular client and she is bringing her dog in a little later than usual today, so I can squeeze your dog in." In this way you are impressing on the caller that you do have appointments, that you are busy and that it is a favor to do his dog on short notice.

If you really do not have the time to do a last-minute caller's dog, by all means offer another time. Perhaps you could fit that dog into your schedule tomorrow. In any event, let the caller know that you appreciate the call and that you do want his business. Remember that without clients you have no business. Even though you may be booked solid and cannot fit in another dog all week, at least be gracious enough to speak kindly to the caller. If the last-minute caller can't accept an appointment for a later date, then thank him for his call and express that you hope to be of service to him in the future.

A few people will always wait and call the groomer at the last minute. These will fit into the "do them if you have time" category. Some of these callers will get angry if you don't have time to take their dogs on short notice. Don't let this bother you. Be pleasant, but keep in mind that these people don't make up the bulk of your business and that your first obligation is to those clients who are your regulars.

WALK-INS

Some shops absolutely do not do walk-in grooming. Whether or not you choose to pursue such a policy will be strictly up to you. It is of course one way to help build up a new business. Sometimes an owner will bring in a dog to be groomed so late in the day that you could not possibly complete it by closing time. The best course to pursue here is to suggest that the dog be brought in on the following day or whenever you have an opening. It is not a good idea to start right off with a new client by staying hours past closing time. This leaves the impression that you have so little to do that you are downright grateful for any crumb of business. Maybe that is true, but you don't want to give that impression to the client. It is strange but true that people would rather patronize the most popular shop in town even if it means waiting for an appointment than to have their dog done immediately at a less-busy and less-popular salon. Somehow, it seems that the busier your shop is, the more attractive it will be to the prospective client. If you have time and wish to do walk-ins, you may want to advertise the fact. A simple line in your advertising will do: "Walk-ins Welcome." If you do not wish to do grooming on this basis, the "Grooming by Appointment Only" sign on your door will make that fact clear.

It can be a little more difficult to turn away a walk-in than it is to turn away a last-minute caller. The owner who walks into your place of business may be able to see that you are not really busy at all and will be offended by your refusal to groom his pet. The only mitigating circumstance might be the time element. Most people are able to understand if you will explain that the amount of time it will take to groom the dog is greater than the amount of time left until closing.

BUDGETING YOUR TIME

A time budget is going to be just as important to you as your financial budget. If you are not careful, you could find that your life is being run by your business rather than the other way around. Small-business owners often find that they are spending far more time than they should in running their business. This is especially true in a service-type business such as dog grooming.

At the very beginning you will need to outline the hours you plan to spend at your place of business. You need to be realistic in your planning. If you choose to work on Saturday, perhaps you will wish to be closed on Sunday and Monday. Whatever days and hours your schedule calls for should be the hours that you actually spend there. Of course, there will be some exceptions, but try to make those exceptions few. If you are not specific in your hours, if you do not adhere to them, you are likely to find yourself at your grooming salon from a very early hour in the morning until a very late hour at night with little time for yourself in between. Try to keep firmly fixed in your mind that one of the reasons for opening your own business was so that you would have some control over the hours and days you worked. Remember the attraction of being able to arrange your own schedule and of being able to have a vacation when you wanted it?

When your business is new and perhaps struggling to get on its feet, the temptation is there to make any accommodation to a customer rather than possibly lose that customer's business. This is an insidious trap and one that eventually could cause you to lose out entirely. If the customer is made to think that you are willing to do his dog any time he desires, then that is exactly what he will expect in the future. The client will have no respect for your hours and indeed will be offended that you would dare to refuse his wishes. If you have made it a practice to come in to your shop so that Mr. X could drop off his dog at 6:30 A.M. on the way to work, you may be sure that Mr. X will be greatly irritated if you later announce that your hours are 8:00 A.M. to 5:00 P.M. and that he will have to wait until 8 to drop off his dog. This is also true of last-minute scheduling. It is very important to have last-minute callers understand that you are taking their dog as an exception and that you normally must have an appointment. If you do not follow this practice, each day will find you hoping that you will have several last-minute callers to fill in your day. You will also find that after one or two visits without an appointment, it will be far more difficult for you to get the client to set up the standing appointment that is so important to your business.

If you will be working alone in your shop, you may wish to have all the dogs come in at the opening of the day and then just call the owners as the dogs are ready to go home. Another way to do this is to have a morning group and an afternoon group of dogs. You might wish to ask all the morning clients to come in between 8 and 8:30 A.M. All these would probably be ready to go home between noon and 1:00 P.M. You could then arrange for all the afternoon dogs to arrive between 12:30 and 1:30. In this way you can avoid having to leave your work repeatedly to accept the next appointment to arrive.

How you arrange your schedule will vary greatly with your circumstances. If you are alone, you will be acting as receptionist and bather as well as groomer. You will have to plan your appointments in such a way that you are able to fill all these functions gracefully. If you do not, you are likely to find that you fall further and further behind as the day progresses. The result, of course, being that you will tend to be more and more irritable and jumpy as the day goes on. This situation is not an enviable one. It is important that you have a firm and reasonable grasp on the extent of your own abilities. Far better (especially at the beginning) to allow yourself too much time rather than too little. It will not be of benefit to you or to your budding business if you are working under such constant pressure that you begin to do sloppy work or to make mistakes.

If you are able to have someone help you in your shop, you will be able to plan your schedule in an entirely different way. With two people in the shop it is quite feasible to schedule appointments for specific times because then you may expect that one or the other of the groomers will be available to bring the dogs in as they arrive.

It is important to allow yourself time for things other than grooming. Don't forget that you are no longer simply an employee who can expect a paycheck at the end of the week. You are the business owner and will have many other jobs within your business besides that of grooming dogs. You will be in charge of ordering supplies, dealing with salespeople who come to call (usually at an inconvenient time), you will be the chief of quality control, scheduling hours and all the other details that go into the running of a business. Some groomers are appalled and disillusioned at all the other tasks that suddenly fall to them when they open their own business. Don't be daunted by these tasks. They are certainly things that must be done, but by planning your schedule well from the very beginning you will be able to deal with all the things that need doing and still have ample time for yourself.

It is important to set your priorities and to stick to them. For most groomers the first order of business is the grooming of dogs. The second may well be janitorial work. While that may sound a bit odd to you, a shop that is not kept clean soon loses business. No one wants to go into a place of business that is dirty and smelly, and without adequate janitorial work a grooming shop is inclined to become smelly in a hurry. Your next order of business may be all the detail work—appointments, reminders and things of that nature. Record keeping is something you must not neglect. Of course, there are always the bills to pay and so forth. You will know what paperwork is pertinent to your own business. Even if you hire a bookkeeper or an accountant you will have to do a certain amount of record keeping.

In setting your working hours, you may wish to set aside one morning or one afternoon a week just for your paperwork. As a general rule, you will find that it is a little easier to set aside a morning than an afternoon. You can simply state that your shop does not open until noon on that day. No one needs to know that you are there and working in your own little office space. This is sometimes a little easier than closing early on a specific day of the week.

You should allow yourself enough time daily to do a good job of cleaning up before the day is done. If you are neat in your working habits, you will find that it won't take too much time to put things away, sweep and damp mop before you go home. In this way, you will come in to find a nice clean shop each morning and so will your customers. At least once each week you will want to plan time for thorough cleaning. If you can afford to hire a janitorial service to come in one evening a week, you will be more than glad that you did. You will free yourself of a lot of drudgery and will be able to maintain that fresh appearance with a minimum of effort.

Vacations

Plan your vacation time. From the very first day you open your doors, know when you will be going on your vacation. If you choose to take the last week in August, that is just fine. If you prefer to take the week after Christmas, that is fine too. Just know when it is to be, write it into your appointment book and don't be swayed from the dates you have chosen by customers who say they just "have" to have their dog done that very week. If your plans are made, you will be able to schedule all your appointments around the time you plan to be gone and your business will go right on smoothly. If you allow yourself to be pulled first one way and then the other by the desires of your clients, then you may never have another vacation.

The week between Christmas and New Year is usually a very slow period in most grooming shops and could be one of the best choices for a vacation time. Another slow period is the entire month of August because people return home from their own vacations then and prepare to get the children back in school. Budgets at this time tend to be tight and grooming drops to a slow pace.

One time frame during which it would be most unwise to schedule your vacation time is the first three weeks of December. This also holds true for the time just prior to any holiday, but especially the Christmas season. People who do not have their pets groomed at any other time of the year will plan to have them all dolled up for Christmas. Even those people who normally do most of their own grooming often will indulge their pet in a trip to the doggy salon just before this special holiday.

It is necessary to plan your vacation time well in advance so that you may begin arranging those all-important standing appointments well ahead of the time you will be away. Keep in mind that while your vacation time is vitally important to you, to the client it is of no importance whatsoever.

A Visual Aid to Time Planning

To help you make up your work schedule or time budget, you will need a large sheet of paper and a notebook. Begin with the notebook. In it you should list your regular chores other than dog grooming. This will include all sorts of paperwork, janitorial duties and so forth. Do not include personal items such as housework, changing the oil in the car or mowing the lawn. Beside each item, estimate how much time you will spend on this chore each day or each week. You should be able to break your various tasks down into categories. Some things will need to be done daily, such as sweeping and mopping floors, while other things can be done once a week, and still others need attention no more often than once a month.

Next, divide your sheet of paper into blocks to represent your calendar for a full month. Divide each working day into morning and afternoon sections. Now you can see how you will be able to develop a visual image of your working schedule. Fill in the once-a-month tasks, such as paying bills and other similar tasks. As you can see, this will only be a very small block of your time. Next, find a time for the weekly tasks. If you need to allot a special time to doing thorough cleaning, determine the amount of time needed and block that in. Maybe on Friday you will want to spend an hour sending reminder cards to all of the customers whose dogs will be coming in week after next. Perhaps you will need one hour sometime during the week for your bookkeeping tasks. For some of these office chores, perhaps you would prefer to come in one hour before your scheduled opening hour so that you may work uninterrupted. Think now of setting aside a regular hour each week and using it for weekly and monthly office work.

Now block in the daily tasks and the amount of time you will need to accomplish those tasks. Daily cleaning chores for instance will probably take up the last thirty minutes of your day. This may be another chore you would prefer to do without the interruptions of regular business, so you may choose to do this after your regular closing hour.

Don't be daunted if your schedule appears to be awfully full without yet having filled in a single hour of dog grooming. This is only a rough draft of your working schedule. As you progress in your business, you will soon learn just how much time you can allocate to each of your chores. The reason for working on this projected schedule is so that you can get an idea of how your time needs to be used.

One of the major problems involved in owning your own business is that of time management. This is especially true if you have always worked as an employee and have not had the responsibility for time planning. It is important for you to learn early in your independent career how to make good use of your time.

Setting Your Hours

In planning your time use, remember that you will need some time that is uninterrupted and that other tasks must fit into several time slots, to be accomplished piecemeal. Those tasks that demand your total concentration might best be planned for times either before your opening hour or after your closing hour. Don't think that because some of your work is done prior to opening or after closing that you must work a twelve-hour day. Even though you will want to cater to the needs of your clientele, don't neglect your own needs. If you want to stay open late one night per week or open on Saturday, then take time off some other day. If you choose to stay open late on Tuesday, then perhaps you will open late on Wednesday, or you might wish to open late on the day you plan to keep evening hours. Any sort of time arrangement that suits you and that seems to work well for your particular clientele should be perfectly all right. If you find that a substantial part of your business is done on Saturday, then you might wish to have Sunday and Monday as your own "weekend." If it is not important to you to have one of the days of the weekend as one of your days off, then feel free to move your own weekend to the middle of the week. Take off Tuesday and Wednesday and keep your shop open on both Saturday and Sunday. This is one of the nice things about being in business for yourself. You can tailor your schedule to fit your own needs and to earn the maximum amount of money for the amount of time you work.

A word of caution about days off and the hours you elect to keep. Please remember that you will never be able to please everyone unless you choose to stay open twenty-four hours a day, seven days a week. No matter what day you have as your day off, someone is going to say that that is absolutely the only day they can bring in their pet. Don't you believe it. Choose your days and your hours and stick to them. You will be surprised at how flexible your clients can be. What you must realize is that if you made an exception for every single client, you would soon find that you were in fact on call every hour of every day and would quickly work yourself into a state of total exhaustion.

If you have elected to open your grooming salon at your home, it is more important than ever that you set your hours and adhere to them. If you possibly can, have a separate business phone with a number different from your home telephone. By all means, invest in a telephone-answering device and when you have reached the close of your business day, switch on the answering machine and let the machine take all calls. If you cannot afford an answering machine at first, then simply unplug your business phone at the end of your working day.

It is especially important for you to post business hours when you are working at your home. Be sure that there is a neat sign prominently displayed so that those people who "just dropped by" will realize you are closed for the day. No, you won't really lose any business this way. Or, more properly, you will not lose any important business this way. The people who are offended by the fact that you wish to keep regular hours are also going to be offended if you do not cater to their every wish, and this type of client is not the backbone of your business.

It will be a little easier to make your hours known and respected if you have a separate shop entrance as was mentioned before. If your home is separated from your shop at all, you can easily post a sign near the shop entrance, then simply do not answer the door at the shop. There will be some people who will persist and will ring your doorbell on the family entrance. It may be difficult for you at first, but you must cultivate the habit of saying politely but firmly that you are sorry, but the shop is closed for the day. Invent some excuse if necessary, but do not even make an appointment after hours. After all, if your shop were located elsewhere, would this individual come to your home after closing hours seeking special services? Not likely.

Those people who have their grooming shops at home have some advantages, but the setting of a time schedule can be a real problem. It is easier to lock the door and go home at 6 o'clock if home is a few blocks away. When home is right next door, the temptation is there to "just this once" stay a little late or make that after-hours appointment. Don't give in. Set up your schedule and stick to it just as if your salon were an hour's drive from your home. You will ultimately be glad that you did and your clients will respect you for respecting yourself.

The other half of setting a time schedule is being on time. If your shop is scheduled to open at 9:00 A.M., then it should open on the dot of 9, not 9:15. If you expect your clients to respect your time, then you must respect theirs. This also holds true for your closing hour. Do not leave early just because you were finished with your work for the day. It will be to your advantage to stay open so that you can receive calls or talk to people who may stop in to make an appointment.

Part of respecting your clients' time is having the dog ready at the time you have said it would be ready, and another part is having the shop open at the regularly scheduled time. Part of your professionalism is being on time and that includes opening on time and closing on time.

Once you have roughed in a basic time schedule, you will probably want to go back and rearrange it. It may take several tries before it works out just right, and what looked just marvelous on paper may prove to be faulty in practice. The major benefit in planning a time schedule is in learning the discipline involved in sticking to a concrete schedule.

Even though you need the discipline involved in keeping on schedule you must learn to be flexible, within reason. Certain tasks can be postponed if time is short. Other tasks must be done on time and it is critical for you to develop a good sense of priorities.

A last word about opening and closing hours. If you decide to change your business hours, be sure to make your plans well in advance and to let your customers know. Post signs at least eight weeks ahead of the projected change and be sure to mention the changes to your regular customers so they will not be taken by surprise.

9

Of Course I Remember Hannibal . . .

Setting Up and Using a Card File

PERHAPS THERE EXISTS somewhere a dog groomer or a beautician who keeps no record whatever of the various clients who come for services, but he or she must be a rarity indeed. It is hard to imagine a dog groomer or a grooming salon without a reference file of some kind that is used to keep track of the various dogs who come in and the services rendered them.

Your file of customers can prove an invaluable resource, without which your business is not likely to thrive. Remember that your clients need to feel special. Remember the tendency of each client to think that he is in fact your only client. The judicious use of a card file for your client dogs can be a valuable tool. With this tool ready to come to your aid, you can make each and every one of your clients feel just as special as they would like to feel, and at the same time you can increase your business and enjoy a reputation as the most caring groomer in town.

FILE TYPES

Your card file could be as unassuming as a shoe box you have covered with bright paper, or it could be as elaborate as a heavy-duty-metal file case. Whatever form it takes, your client file is an important part of your business and should be kept close at hand.

Most salons find keeping the file next to the telephone at the reception desk is ideal. This allows for quick reference when a client calls in.

A few groomers use three-by-five-inch cards and a small recipe-type file box for storage. These will do if nothing else is available (and are certainly better than no files at all) but this size card is very limiting because it greatly inhibits the amount of information that can be entered.

Probably the most practically sized card for your record-keeping purposes is the five-by-seven-inch lined file card. This is a standard size and is readily available at any office-supply store, and in a pinch can sometimes be found in the stationery departments at other stores as well. There are available several different types of file boxes that will hold these cards neatly and keep them readily at hand. One sort of file box is inexpensive cardboard. It is reasonably durable and can be made quite attractive if you wish to cover it with a bright contact paper. Covering this kind of file box with contact paper will also make the file sturdier and help it to last longer. These boxes come in a plain woodgrain finish that is quite acceptable just as it is. The inside of this kind of file box has a metal slide that holds the cards in place.

The same size cards will also fit nicely into a file box like the one just mentioned but made of metal. Naturally this is considerably more expensive. These are of course much more durable than the cardboard boxes, but they fulfill the same function. They do come in a variety of finishes and are generally very respectable and businesslike in appearance with no additional covering. They can be enhanced with small decals if you wish to dress them up so that they fit in better with your office decor.

One way to acquire metal file boxes at a greatly reduced price is to check the various second-hand stores in your neighborhood. You might also look around in a military-surplus store because these files are in common use in military offices. If you do find a file box in the size you need at a military-surplus store, it will likely be a very unattractive shade of olive green. These boxes can be painted with any good enamel paint or can be covered with contact paper just as you might cover the cardboard file.

SETTING UP YOUR FILING SYSTEM

Once you have acquired a file box and a supply of cards, you are ready to set up your filing system. Only one other item is needed for good organization and that is a set of alphabetized file dividers. These are not an absolute requirement, but as you will see, they will certainly simplify your filing system.

One of the simplest yet most efficient ways to organize your filing system is to use an alphabetical system based on the last name of the dog owner. When using a system of this type, the easiest way to set up the cards for the file is to list the last name of the dog owner, followed by his first name. This information is recorded on the upper left corner of the card. In the upper right corner of the card, list the name of the dog. Thus the top line on the card might read: *Smith, Mary ——— Fluffy*. On the second line, begin on the left with the address and telephone number. This can be followed by the breed, sex and age of the dog. The second line then might read: *222 W. 2nd St., 555-1212 — Poodle, 3 yrs., F.*

If you plan to require proof of immunizations for dogs coming into your salon, this information could be recorded on the third line on the card. Because it is important that this information be kept current, be sure to list the date when the last immunizations were given so that you will be able to tell when they should be repeated. Thus line three might read: *1-1-84   Rabies, DHL, Parvo*. This still will leave space for several updates on the same line. You may wish to skip line four so that the immunization record can be continued. If you wish, you can also make the immunization record on a separate card. This can then be attached to the regular card. If you choose to do this, you might want to list the dog's veterinarian and phone number also. The major disadvantage to using a separate card for each dog is that it will fill your file box more quickly.

Line five can now begin your actual grooming record on this particular dog. On the left side of the card indicate the month, day and year followed by the services required, and end on the right side with a total charge for this visit. Line five might look something like this: *1-1-85 — Bath, Clip Nails, Blow Dry. $22.00*.

There are so many ways to record the various services rendered in a grooming shop that pages and pages could be devoted to the different listings. Suffice it to say that whatever way you choose to record those services should be consistent and should be something you will be able to decipher at a later date. Your card file will not be nearly as valuable a tool for your business if it is written in such a way that even you are unable to decipher its meaning at a later date.

Abbreviations are perfectly all right and can be very useful. They save writing time and space on the card. Just try to stick with the same form so there won't be any confusion at a later time. If you intend to use BB to indicate a bath and blow dry, then let it indicate a bath and blow dry every single time you use that abbreviation. Don't use it on another occasion to indicate a bath and brush. See how easy it might be to confuse yourself? Try to keep in mind that someday you may have someone working for you who will need to be able to read your file cards just as accurately as you do. If you will keep that firmly in mind from the very beginning of your record keeping, you will always have a file that is a real working asset to your business.

It is important for you to be sure to record each and every visit made by a particular dog. In this way, you can keep close track of just what you have done for this client, how much you charged for the services and how often this dog usually comes in for grooming. It can be embarrassing not to remember that your client was just in two weeks ago. If your card file is updated at every single visit this need never happen.

When recording a visit by a particular dog, be sure to note any sort of problem you may have discovered, and record also what was done about that problem. If the notation reads "ticks," it would also be necessary to show that a dip was given to the dog (and charged for) and what product was used. The next time the owner calls in, you can refer quickly to the card and ask if they have had any more problems with ticks. This certainly makes it appear as if you have a super memory and are really interested in this particular dog. (In addition to these benefits, you can also determine the effectiveness of the products you are using.) If you discovered some problem that needed medical attention, the owner will certainly be pleased if you inquire about his pet's health. Of course, if the dog has not been taken to see the veterinarian, that fact will be established also. In that way, you will avoid being blamed for some problem that was present when the dog arrived at your shop.

If there were extra charges on any visit, be sure that the various items are listed separately so that you do not inadvertently overcharge the next time the dog comes in for grooming. For instance, if there was a special charge for a severely matted dog, you might simply note the fact and the charges in this way: *mats—$4.50, grooming—$18.00.* Then the total amount would appear on the far right side of the card: *$22.00.* This lets you know that the dog would

A preprinted record card allows the groomer to keep complete records on each client's dog.

A five-by-seven-inch lined card can be used to record important information about each animal.

normally only cost $18.00 but that on this visit you had extra work to do in combing out a matted coat and thus charged an extra fee. Do be sure that you explain extra charges to the client in advance so that there is no surprise at the time the dog is picked up. Also, it is nice to remind the owner at the time of payment what the normal fee would be. In this way, you will prevent misunderstandings and you will not frighten the client at the prospect of paying the larger amount at every visit.

If by some chance you have several clients whose names are exactly the same, then of course you would further break down the alphabetizing according to the dogs' names. In the event that one client has several dogs, all the cards would be filed together and would further be alphabetized by the name of each dog. If you wish, you may indicate by the use of a number at the very top of the card that this client is a multiple-dog owner. This would simplify finding several cards, or would allow you to ask which of the dogs was coming for a visit if the owner failed to mention the dog he was bringing in on this date.

Having that card file in close proximity to your telephone can be one of the biggest helps you will have in your business. It allows you to see at a glance just what the entire picture is on any given dog. If, for instance, a client calls in for an appointment on a day when your time is limited and you can see from the information listed on the card that this dog is almost always severely matted and requires extra grooming time, you will know that you may not have time for that dog on the day requested, and you can then suggest a different day when you will have more time available. Your card file will also allow you to know, without having to ask the client, exactly what was done for this particular dog on his last visit or on his last several visits. All of this information can be a big help to you in knowing what will be done at the next visit, and will allow you to make your plans accordingly.

As you can see, even this most simple of filing systems will help you make better use of your time and will also help you please your customers more by apparently remembering their dog each time they call for an appointment. There are other and more complicated file systems you might use, but none is really much more efficient than that outlined here. Some people will use different-color pens to indicate various things and some may use rather elaborate codes, but, in the end, whatever works well for you will prove to be the best possible system. Keep your filing system simple, logical, complete and up-to-date and you will find that your file is indeed one of your best business friends.

Special Uses

It cannot be stressed too strongly that it is important to keep your filing system up-to-date and correct. If a client moves or changes telephone numbers, it will help you to know that fact. You might make it a habit to verify the basic information at frequent intervals because you will be able to use your file for more than just recording the visits made by each dog. It is necessary to verify the information frequently because owners will simply forget to tell you about any changes and you are likely to be caught unaware.

Remember the chapter when standing appointments were discussed? If you will recall, mention was made that your client was very likely going to forget that appointment. Here is one way in which your filing system can help you. About eight to ten days in advance of an appointment, you may wish to send out reminder cards. You can have these printed up in such a way that they only require a minimum of writing on your part to fill in the necessary information. Here is a very real reason to be sure that the information on the card is current. It will do you little good to send a postcard to an incorrect address. Not only will you miss reminding the client of his dog's appointment, but you will have wasted the postage as well. In your own business you cannot afford to be wasteful because you will soon discover that wasted money is a part of your profits.

With regard to telephone numbers, if a client mentions to you that he has an unlisted (sometimes called "nonpublished") number, it will be wise for you to make a note of that fact on the card. This will let you (and any of your employees) know that should someone call and request this client's number, you are not free to give it out. It is unwise, in fact, to give any information about your clients without their prior approval.

Your card file can also help you to build your business through follow-up calls. If you have recommended veterinary care for a dog, you might wish to call the client in three or four days and make an inquiry about the dog's progress. This makes a nice impression on the client—you actually cared enough about his dog to take the time to call and ask about its health.

If an animal has been treated with a product for external parasites and you are not sure whether or not this product is doing its job, then by all means contact the clients whose pets were treated and ask if the product was effective. This again will show your clients just how concerned you are about the dogs who come to your salon, and how careful you are to see that the products you are using are adequate. Your concern makes every client feel special, and when your clients are made to feel special, you can be sure they will send all their friends to your shop.

More Uses for Your File

In your business, it is inevitable that you will get calls requesting information about stud service, pups and all manner of other things. One of the ways you can render services of this nature is to have a simple index of dog breeds and list under each breed the names of your clients who own dogs of that breed. You will almost certainly know whether a client is or is not interested in using his male dog for stud service. If, by some chance, you are not sure, it might be thoughtful of you to call the client yourself and ask permission before referring someone. Some of your clients may prefer that their telephone numbers not be released for that purpose. It is also very common for a groomer to know whether a particular client has pups available for sale. Again, do be sure that your client wants to have callers referred to him. He may have already placed all the pups from this litter and would find calls an annoyance.

This would be an opportune time to make some observations in regard to referrals. Whether or not you choose to make referrals is certainly your own choice. If you do choose to make referrals, be well aware that the outcome of those referrals can certainly reflect on you. If one of your clients sells a sick pup to someone you have referred, you may be quite sure that the person who bought the pup will tell all his friends just where he learned about this litter. The reverse is also true. If the buyer is especially pleased with the pup he located because of your referral, you will certainly be praised for having sent the buyer to just the right breeder. If you know your clients well, and are fairly sure they are selling sound, healthy pups or that they have a really fine stud dog, then by all means do make the referral. If you have any doubts at all about the quality or health of the dogs in question then you might wish to say nothing at all. It is better to say nothing than to make a less-than-positive statement

the Groomery

DOGPATCH

939 Hauoli Street
At the 1800 block South King Street
Honolulu, HI 96826 · Tel. 945-7778 · Open 7 days

Name of Pet	
Name of Owner	
Address	
Telephone	

SERVICES INCLUDE:	Charges
Grooming	
Bath	
Ear Cleaning	
Nail Clipping	
Flea Treatment	
Medicated Bath	
In-Home Grooming	
Quarantine Care	
Show Coat Conditioning	
Boarding	
Conformation Handling	
Canine Modeling	
Delivery	
Comments	Subtotal
	Tax
	Total

Signature   Date

Another type of preprinted form, this grooming slip is meant to serve as both information for the groomer and a statement of charges for the owner.

137

about the breeder. If you are pressed for an opinion about a breeder you do not wish to recommend, you can feel free to simply say, "I'm sorry, that is not one of the breeders to whom I send referrals." Let the would-be buyer draw his own conclusions from that. It is astounding how the buyer can hold you responsible for a referral gone sour. It can also affect your credibility and your business reputation for the worse.

If you are familiar with reputable dog breeders in your area and are comfortable with the quality of the pups or stud service being offered, then by all means make recommendations as you see fit to those who call. This is an area in which you will have to use your own judgment based on your knowledge of the area and the situation at hand.

One way to protect yourself to some extent in matters of this nature is to make sure that you inform the caller that you are only giving him the information so that he may check it for himself and that you are not in any way endorsing the pups or the stud in question. This is of some help should the caller be dissatisfied with a puppy he might acquire as a result of your recommendations. If you have made this kind of disclaimer, you can feel free to remind the buyer that you did not suggest that he make the purchase and that your only involvement was to inform him of the availability of the litter. Of course, you are not actually responsible for the quality of pups you might know of, but the fact that you made a recommendation will lead the buyer to feel that you are in some way responsible for the people to whom you make referrals. In fact, some buyers will believe that you are getting a fee for your referrals and no amount of argument will convince them otherwise.

You should be aware also that many buyers have unreasonable expectations of the pups they purchase, and they will tend to blame the breeder, the person who made the referral to that particular breeder or anyone else they can find rather than accept responsibility for their own poor choice or poor management. This is especially true when the dog in question turns out to have some sort of behavior problem. Often the problem is strictly one of the buyer's own making, but he is certainly going to try to place the blame elsewhere.

In addition to providing you with a ready reference for referrals, your card file will also provide you with an instant mailing list you can use for a variety of purposes. At Christmas time, you may wish to use this as your Christmas-card list. Some groomers send the card to the dog in care of the owner. You will be surprised at how pleased some owners seem to be with this sort of gesture. You might also send doggy birthday cards or an anniversary card on the anniversary of a dog's first visit to your salon.

If you are running a promotional special of some sort, your card file can help you to zero in on just those clients who might be especially interested in this special service. If you are having a discount on terriers for instance, the Poodle owners among your clients will not be interested, but all your terrier owners will appreciate being informed that they can have a discount during this time. This helps your advertising reach the group of clients most likely to respond and most interested in this special offer. You will save on your expenses by mailing only to those likely to be interested and you can also expect a higher percentage of responses, so your advertising dollars are used to best advantage. The greater the percentage of response, the greater your percentage of profit.

Depending on your circumstances and the services you plan to offer, you will probably develop other uses for your card file as you become more adept at using it. It is important for you to get in the habit of maintaining a good record from the very beginning. You will be surprised at how much information you will amass about your various client dogs and you will also be surprised at how often the owners will ask you to answer questions about their pet. One item that comes to mind is the question of seasons. Always note when a female dog is in season. If, six weeks later, this dog comes in looking as if it might be expecting pups, you can make sure to check with the owner before administering a dip. Perhaps the client simply forgot to inform you that the dog was expecting pups. Often owners are not aware that expectant mothers should not be given any sort of dip. You might save the owner from losing pups due to having the mother exposed to toxic chemicals. The owner will be grateful you cared enough to take the dog's welfare seriously. Again, good record keeping has made you look completely professional and extraordinarily caring. This can only be of benefit to your business.

Another of the special uses you will probably wish to put your card file to is to indicate urgent priority information about each individual animal. Here is one place where a bright red felt marker will come in handy. For instance, if a particular animal is sensitive to a certain dip, you will wish to note that fact in large red letters so that you and any of your employees will be well aware that it could be very dangerous to use that product on this dog.

If your client tells you that his dog has a heart problem, you will wish to mark the card so that you will be extra careful not to place this dog in any kind of stress situation. This could mean the difference between life and death for some pets and you certainly would prefer that the dog not have a heart attack while in your care.

Naturally, you are concerned with the welfare of every dog that comes into your shop. You are also concerned with your own welfare. Dogs who are of extremely bad disposition can be hazardous to your health and you will perhaps wish to note simply *bites* at the top of the card. If you feel that the owner might be offended should he see such a notation, then you may wish to make up some sort of code to let you know that this dog could be a problem. The simple letter *B* in red on the top of the card could be enough to alert you to the fact that this dog is not thrilled with your attentions, or perhaps a diagonal red slash across one corner of the card will call to mind this animal's behavior problems. Many owners like to believe that their dog would never be unruly, and you may well wish to go along with those beliefs in the interest of good customer relations.

UPDATING YOUR CARD FILE

From time to time it will be necessary for you to weed out some of the cards from your file. At first, you will have no idea which of the people who come in will be your regular clientele and which will be one-time visitors. Much as you would like to have every new client become a regular patron of your business, you must realize that it is virtually impossible for you to please all of the people all of the time and some of the people who come in one time will never be back. Others will come once or twice and then decide to patronize another shop.

There are any number of reasons that might cause a client to stop coming into your place of business. One reason of course would be that the client no longer owns the dog that came in for your services. This may come about because the dog has died, been stolen or lost, or because the owner has sold or given the dog away. It is possible that you might have somehow given offense to the owner or perhaps a change in the owner's economic circumstances dictates that dog grooming is a luxury that just does not fit into his budget. As a business owner, you must be aware of the reasons that might cause you to lose a customer. If the cause is one you are able to remedy, then by all means take steps to correct the problem. If the reason for losing a customer is not something over which you can exercise control, then don't take the loss as a personal affront.

For about the first year or even two years you have your salon open, you will probably keep every card in your record. After that time frame, you will probably wish to make a periodic weeding out of your card file. This will make sure that the file is an active working file and that the majority of the cards pertain to those clients who are actually patronizing your place of business.

There are several ways to clear the deadwood from your card file. One way of course, is simply to discard any card on a client dog that has not been in for grooming within a certain period of time. With most breeds, any dog that has not been in for a visit within, say, a six-month period might well be considered an inactive client. If you have reason to believe that this animal is one of those who only comes in for pre-Christmas grooming, then you will probably wish to leave the card in your active file for at least a full year.

You may want to discard these information cards entirely or you might prefer simply to place them in an inactive file. You will be surprised at how long it can take between visits for some clients. Not surprisingly, the client expects you to recall, as if it were yesterday, exactly what was done for the dog on his last visit even though that visit was over two years ago. When a client calls and you are unable to find his name in your active file, it will be wise to verify whether his dog has been to your salon before. If the answer is yes, ask how long ago. Then you should be able to go to the inactive file, pull the card in question and amaze and delight the client by recalling all about his dog and the last time it was in for grooming.

Even the inactive file can be weeded out every so often. You may feel fairly confident that any animal that has not been in within two or three years is probably not going to be coming back. As with anything else, there are exceptions to this generality. If you are in business in an area with a military installation you may find that you will have clients who will depart the area, be absent for two or three years (or even more) and come right back to your salon when they return to this particular area.

When checking through your files, if you want to be certain that an owner still has the dog in question, you may wish to send out a card to that owner, reminding him that it has been some time since you were able to serve his grooming needs and inviting him in for some sort of special offer, such as a percentage off on his dog's next grooming. Another way to check is simply to make a phone call to the owner and ask if he still owns the dog. Sometimes you will find that the owner has moved or no longer has a dog at all. Then you can feel free to throw that particular card away.

Keeping your card file updated and viable is one way to keep a check on the growth of your business. A survey of the card file can help you keep tabs on the percentage of repeat business you are achieving, and you can get a very close estimate on the average frequency of visits for the various breeds that are groomed at your shop. All this information can be used to help you promote your business to its best advantage.

All in all, the card file is the very heartbeat of the dog groomer's business. It is a close indicator of the success you are having and can easily help you to head off a potential problem if you see that your repeat business is lessening. Perhaps you are neglecting to ask the client to make that repeat appointment, perhaps you are not reminding him of the appointment, perhaps you have left some need unfilled and the client chose to go elsewhere. Any of these things can have an effect on your business success or failure.

Make it a habit to scan your file from time to time and make yourself aware of the course your business is taking. You will find that this is time well spent.

10

Reading between the Lines . . .

The Customer Is Not Always Right

IF THERE IS just one area that can make or break any grooming salon in the world (or for that matter any service-related business whatsoever) that area is customer relations and communication. In so many businesses the motto is "the customer is always right," and the customer has come to believe that he is in fact always right. Unfortunately, this is not necessarily the case. The general public is so woefully uninformed with regard to the needs of their dogs that it would very likely be the exception rather than the rule that the customer is always right at the dog-grooming shop.

The question of who *is* right at the grooming shop becomes a very touchy subject. Some people project their own feelings on their dogs. Many attribute to their pets the ability to reason in a human way and they simply are not well enough informed to be able to make sound judgments with regard to the welfare of their dogs. The owner, however, most assuredly does not wish to have a dog groomer (or anyone else for that matter) tell him that he just doesn't know what he is talking about. The only people who might get away with that sort of statement would be physicians. Most people, unfortunately, do not view dog groomers as the well-trained professional people that they are. This is likely to remain the case until dog grooming becomes the sort of profession that requires school training and state licensing. Because your clients are unlikely to view you as a fully professional individual who is well able to make a good judgment with regard to the needs and welfare of dogs, you will have to deal with this problem from a slightly different angle.

The longer you are in this business, the more awareness you are sure to develop about just how emotional people become about their pets. It is important to keep this fact in mind when you are dealing with your customers. It is very easy to offend a customer by implying that he doesn't know what he is talking about. Once you have offended the client, you have probably lost his business and you may well have lost the business of several of his friends. It is going to be important to your business that you learn early in your career how best to handle some of the problems you are likely to face in dealing with a largely uninformed and highly emotional clientele.

WHY DO PEOPLE OWN DOGS?

To help you understand how your client looks upon his dog, let's look at the reasons people own pets of any kind and dogs in particular. One of the primary reasons people own pets is to fill an empty space in their emotional life. For the individual who has no children, the dog can become a viable substitute for a child. Keep in mind that every parent likes to think that he is the best judge of the needs of his children. This is also very true of the dog owner whose dog fills that particular need in his life. Other people have children who are grown and no longer dependent and so the dog becomes the substitute for a younger and more dependent child. The dog may also fill the position of obedient child. A parent whose children are out of hand and causing trouble may find great comfort in the company of an amenable dog. All of these people are in a parenting position with the dog in the role of child or infant. Few of these people are really aware of the underlying reason they have chosen to own a dog, and fewer still would appreciate the dog groomer telling them what the reason might be. As a dog groomer, you need only be aware of the situation and its possibilities in order to adapt to it best.

For some people, a dog serves to bolster a sagging ego. This may be especially true of the people who choose to own large aggressive dogs. Often these owners will assure the groomer that "no one can handle him but me." This may or may not be the case. Because you are still dealing with a dog, you will probably be well able to handle the dog—the owner may prove to be a different matter.

Dogs can fill an ego-building need in other ways. For some people, their dog becomes the beauty they feel they lack in their own person. This may express itself in showing the dog in competition or in simply accepting the admiration of other people who think that this is a beautiful dog. This type of owner may assure you that his dog is "pick of the litter" or "from a great line" or "is a perfect specimen of his breed, but we just don't want to show him" or other words of like nature. This owner does not want to hear from you or from anyone else that his dog is less than perfect in any way. You may have to handle certain problems very tactfully or this owner will be deeply offended. With owners of this kind, you must understand that anything you say that could be construed as a negative remark will be taken by the client as a direct reflection on him. He is almost certainly not aware of this situation at all, but he will be sure to prove to be highly defensive of his pet in every way, whether you are referring to the dog's disposition or to the condition of his coat. Even the presence of fleas or ticks may trigger this type of client into a defensive attitude. To this person, a problem of this nature is an admission that he has failed to care for his dog adequately, and because his own ego is so bound up in the dog, he becomes extremely agitated. This client requires very tactful handling.

The third primary reason for owning a dog is to fill the need for companionship. These owners will fall into two subcategories, the first being the person who lacks human companionship for one reason or another and has a dog in lieu of human companions. These clients are indeed likely to view their pets on a most human level and may attribute to them some very highly developed human characteristics. This client may tell you in all seriousness just how his dog feels about various matters. This is a situation that can appear laughable until you realize that the client is not making a joke. He actually believes that he is expressing exactly what his dog feels. In sharing this information with you, the client is placing his trust in you to understand his feelings and to accept them. If you take his remarks lightly or make jokes about his dog's feelings, this client is likely to be hurt as well as offended, and again you risk losing a client.

The second subcategory is the owner who owns a dog for the real pleasure of owning a dog. This client is likely to be among the most sensible of all the clients you have. He tries to understand his dog as a dog. He does not project his own feelings onto his dog to any extent. He may be quite well informed about dogs and their needs or he may not be so well informed. If he is not particularly well informed, this client is one of the few who is probably aware that he has a lot to learn and will be interested in and appreciative of your help and information.

It can be of great benefit to the grooming salon owner to understand some of the primary reasons for dog ownership. Through this understanding, it is possible to deal with clients in such a way that every client feels special and appreciates your care and concern.

CLIENT TYPES

In your business, you will discover that you will be dealing with three basic types of clients. A few of your clients may cross over from one type to another or may not be clearly defined as one particular type, but as a rule you will be able to fit most of your clients into one of these three categories.

The Super Client

The first type of client is the one who is a sheer joy to know. This client cares for his dog and wants him to be well groomed and in good shape. This client is sensible, takes advice when needed and is generally pleasant in every way. This dog owner is the kind who makes your life easy and you could live happily ever after if every one of your clients were from this same mold. Unfortunately, this grade-A super client will be in the minority. You will certainly come to love those you are lucky enough to have in your file who fit this category. Some of these clients may eventually develop into friends as well as business acquaintances. When dealing with a super client, feel free to give him tips about dog care from your own experience whether or not they pertain to grooming. This client is almost always eager to learn and will appreciate your interest in his dog. He is certainly going to profit from the advice you give him.

The Average Owner

The second client category is probably going to make up the bulk of your total clientele. This client is generally pleasant, is somewhat prey to old wives' tales and may or may not be particularly amenable to advice. This client cares enough for his dog to see that it has the basic necessities of care and wants to keep the dog in generally good shape, but well-groomed dogs are not one of his first priorities. This client is really an average individual, more often pleasant than not, but he will occasionally have a bad day and be a bit on the grumpy side. He is going to be more budget conscious than the super client, but will not begrudge a fair price for a good job. He is not overly demanding in his requirements. All in all, these clients are going to be fairly easy to deal with so long as you are willing to make a little effort to accommodate them on their bad days and so long as you show a real interest in them and in their dogs. Like all clients, these folks will be quick to spot insincerity. Take good care of your average clients because they are your bread and butter.

The Impossible Owner

Now we come to the third client category. Like the super client, this type will be very much in the minority among your various clients and you will be most grateful that this is the case, for this is the "impossible" owner. These owners have a chip on their shoulder and know all there is to know about dogs in general and their own dog in particular. If you don't believe it, just ask them. This owner is prone to find fault with everything you do, and everything you say and is not about to take any sort of advice or recommendation from any mere dog groomer. In the eyes of this client, you are little better than a common laborer and probably are out to cheat him in some way. This client is the bane of the salon owner's existence. Unfortunately, this client also tends to be extremely vocal and in some instances may also be prone to lawsuits.

There is virtually no way to know in advance that you are making an appointment for an impossible client. Once in a while, you may get a hint from the first telephone conversation, but this is not a good way to judge and it is not fair to make such a judgment so soon.

When you find yourself with an impossible client on your hands, you are probably going to be most uncomfortable. This client is the kind who will challenge your every statement, question every penny of your charges, insist on special services, demand that you make an appointment on the day of his choice no matter what, and when you have finally done his dog and are really proud of the work, he is likely to find fault with the job you have done. At first, the attitude of the impossible client is likely to cause the shop owner a certain amount of mental anguish. Everything this individual says hits home in a very tender spot—your ego. It is most important that you learn early in your business career that you are not at fault and that the complaints made by this impossible client do not truly reflect on you or your capabilities.

Whether or not you have or can develop a thick enough skin and enough self confidence to deal with the impossible client is a very individual matter. Keep firmly in mind that this client is not a large percentage of your clientele, is not representative of the people with whom you will regularly do business and is not the final authority on your abilities. You are an independent business owner and you are the one to set your own standards. Dealing with this impossible client can take the form of a challenging game if you are of a nature to handle this sort of sparring. To insure your own peace of mind it is important that you are able to mentally brush off the criticism you are sure to get from this individual. If you do not feel comfortable in this kind of oneupmanship situation, you may be better off in not continuing to groom a dog for this kind of client. It is simply going to be too hard on you.

If you have elected to discontinue service to an impossible client, it is important to your good business practices that your "firing" of the client take place in such a way that the client is hardly aware of having been turned away.

When one of these extremely difficult clients has brought a dog in for grooming, you may wish to indicate with some sort of personal coding on the file card that this client is very hard to please. Just how you indicate this is up to you, but tact dictates that commentary that is less than flattering to the customer be in some form not readily discernible should the client chance to glimpse the card. A single letter in the upper right hand corner of the card might make the situation clear at a glance and at the same time give the client no further fuel for his ire. This coded card should be left in the file so that you will be able to refer to it and can avoid inadvertently scheduling a grooming for this client because you might have forgotten your past experience.

One of the easiest ways to discontinue service to a client of this nature is simply not to have an appointment available for this particular dog. Nothing at all. When the client calls, he will almost always wish to choose a date to have his dog groomed. Naturally, you will have developed the habit of inquiring at the outset of any call for grooming: "Have we done your dog before?" Then of course, you will open your file and refer to the card you had made previously. This card indicates by way of your special code that this client is difficult to please. If you do not choose to make another effort to please this client, then a simple and tactful way of avoiding this appointment is simply to have nothing available at the time he wishes to have the dog groomed. Your remark might go something like this, "This Friday, Mrs. Blank? Oh, I am so sorry. We don't have a single thing available for Friday." If the client has made a general request for a particular week rather than for a specific date, you might say, "Goodness, we are just booked solid all that week." Notice that no alternate day or week is suggested. If you actually wished to groom a particular dog and in fact did not have an appointment available on the day or during the week the customer had requested, you might have continued with, "But I do have an opening on Thursday" or, "You know, I could squeeze him in early the week after." With the impossible client, simply do not offer that alternative. Say absolutely nothing. Wait for the client to continue. This is very important. Do not give in and say another word. Just wait. Usually, the client will wait in silence for you to offer an alternate date and when you do make that offer he is ready to do battle to get the date and time he wants. When no alternate date is forthcoming, he is likely to retreat in some confusion. You have been polite, you have been "so sorry," you have given him nothing to fight about and you have not made any sort of counter offer.

In many cases, that will be the end of the whole matter. The impossible client will mutter some close to the conversation and then hang up. You can breathe a sigh of relief and refile the card in case he calls another time. If the client offers an alternate date, you will of course, find that you are simply too busy on that date also and with the same gentle apology offer no other alternate date. You will still await the client's answer. It is seldom necessary for you to go through this script more than two or three times at the most until the client becomes so disgusted that he will choose to take his dog elsewhere. Occasionally, you will have one of these clients become impressed that you are so much in demand you are constantly busy, and he will call in and ask outright for any appointment you may have available. If he does this and is that willing to adapt to your schedule, you may wish to give him one more try. It is an odd phenomenon that some people will make every effort to intimidate those with whom they do business, but upon finding that they are simply refused in a pleasant manner because the business is so very popular, they develop a new respect for the businessperson and can in fact turn out to be clients who will be loyal and supportive.

It is certainly worth your while to give this client one more chance if he has seemed to develop a better attitude. If on the second chance you find that he is just as difficult to deal with as he was initially, then you may wish to make sure never to give him an appointment in the future. Naturally, this will be one instance in which you will not recommend a standing appointment, and will in fact simply refrain from mentioning any future work.

In dealing with the client who is making your life miserable, it is best to remember that you are an independent businessperson and that you do not have to have future dealings with this person. Argument is not worthwhile and no matter what the outcome of an argument, you are ultimately the loser if only in your own mental upset. It is very difficult for the client of this nature to continue his disagreeable behavior if he is not getting an argumentative response from you. If you can learn to say very simply and sincerely, "I am really sorry that you feel that way," you may find that this phrase is one that can help to avoid many confrontations. This is not an argumentative phrase and leaves little for the client to say. It does not put you in the position of having an out-and-out disagreement, but it certainly does not commit you to an admission of any sort. If you feel that some adjustment is in order, by all means offer to make whatever arrangement you consider fair. You will feel better if you can avoid the no-win situation of arguing with a client. The impossible client is unlikely to be satisfied with any arrangement that you can make and you will suffer less mental anguish when you learn simply to reply quietly and vow to yourself never to do business with this individual again. If the client persists in a harangue, ask pleasantly "Mr. X, what can I do to make you happy?" Now the full burden is on the client and you will generally find that he has no real solution.

The Impossible Request

In some cases, you may think that you have an impossible owner on your hands when in fact the only problem is one of communication. Some owners will insist on making requests that are totally impossible and out of the question. Do not be too quick to judge the impossible-request maker as an impossible client. Often these requests are made out of a lack of knowledge and understanding of exactly what dog grooming entails. Keep firmly in your mind the fact that, to your client, you work some sort of magic. Your business is a total mystery to the customer. Most clients have no idea how long it takes to perform any particular service. Some people confuse dog grooming with their own visit to the beauty salon or the barber shop, and find it hard to understand why their dog can't be all done and ready to go home in an hour.

Owners frequently believe that they do good maintenance work on their dog at home and have a really hard time understanding what you mean when you tell them the dog is so severely matted that in kindness to the dog all the hair should be cut off. The owner has no idea how to brush the dog correctly and is appalled at the idea of having his dog "disfigured" by a short haircut. Here is a good example of the kind of impossible request that can be dealt with if you will take the time to explain and show the owner what you are talking about. Show the owner the tools you use and actually demonstrate on a small area just how difficult it is to brush out the matted coat. If you will let the owner make an effort to imitate what you have just done, he will usually understand what you are talking about. Most owners do not wish to cause their dogs physical pain. If the owner remains adamant about having the matted dog brushed out rather than cut, one tactful way to change his mind is to express your regrets that his grooming bill is going to be high and suggest that he can save a sizable portion of that bill if he would like to prebrush the dog and bring it back tomorrow. This suggestion can have some amazing results. Often the customer responds well to your concern over his budget, and will allow you to do what is necessary. In other cases, the owner will attempt to prebrush the dog and will find that it is a far more difficult task than he had anticipated. Usually this client will have quite a change of attitude toward your capability and will respect your judgment far more than he did in the past. If he still insists on the brush-out work, you may wish to simply overestimate the final bill. It may change his mind, but even if it does not, there will be no real surprise when the final bill is rendered.

Another request you will get is the request to do a particular style that is not going to look nice on a dog because of the coat texture or some other factor. In this case, your best bet is to make a serious effort to explain as pleasantly and as tactfully as possible why this is not going to work well for this dog. Some groomers will comply with this kind of request, only to find that the client blames the groomer for the fact that his dog doesn't look as good as the client had expected it to look. You are likely to find this especially true with the owners of some Poodles who have silky, straight coats. This type of coat simply hangs limp and looks awful in the fancy patterns popular for Poodles. The owner will not understand that his dog has a coat that does not lend itself well to this style. One very tactful way to deal with this request is to say something like, "You know, Snowball has such a beautiful silky coat that I'm afraid it isn't going to stand up in this type of pattern. Why don't you let me try this," then give the client a suggestion for a clip you are sure will work well for the coat. The client doesn't know or care that a silky coat is incorrect for a Poodle. If you emphasize something nice about the dog and flatter the owner by doing so, you will generally find that the client is far more amenable to your suggestions than if you are critical of the coat his dog has. While the client does know what the correct coat type is for the breed in question, he is firmly convinced that his dog is the ideal and nothing that you can say is likely to dissuade him from this line of thought. In fact, critical remarks about the client's dog will only risk the loss of an otherwise delightful client.

Once in a while, you will have a request to "Make him look like . . ." followed by a description that is absolutely impossible, given the dog in question. Sometimes, the client has seen some other dog he admired and sometimes the idea is just something that the client has envisioned. As a groomer, you are well aware that some things are virtually impossible. Here is where the maximum possible tact must come into play, and your imagination must really be working overtime. In order to satisfy this kind of impossible request, you must be ready to make the client think you are doing just what he wants, while at the same time you are in fact doing the best you can with what you have to work with. If the request is to make this dog look like a particular breed and the dog (and its coat) bear no resemblance to the breed in question, sometimes it is possible to begin a description of the usual method of grooming for the breed requested and find that is not what the client had in mind at all. This

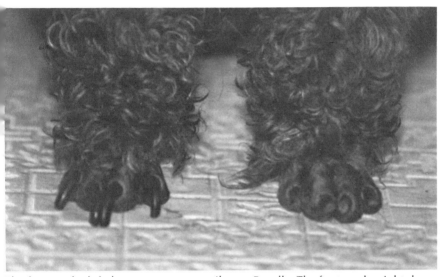

The foot on the left shows overgrown nails on a Poodle. The foot on the right shows the nails trimmed to the correct length.

is an example of an impossible request based solely on the client's lack of knowledge or information. The request in and of itself is in fact quite impossible, but what the client *really* wants may be well within reach.

MAY I WATCH?

Some of your clients will inevitably ask if they may stay and watch while you do their dog. This is of course up to you. It is worth considering however, that most dogs are far more difficult to work with if the owner is present. They keep looking to the owner to get them out of this mess and often the owner is so sympathetic with his pet that little work can be accomplished. Other clients will want to wait in the waiting room. This can have very much the same effect on the dog. He is so busy trying to get back to the owner that the groomer's life becomes a real trial.

A few customers will wish to observe your work in the hope that by doing so they will be able to groom the dog themselves. As you well know, a customer is not going to learn enough to be able to groom his pet at home. All that is likely to happen is that the owner will make a thorough mess of the dog that you will have to correct at a later date.

FIGURING OUT WHAT THE CLIENT *REALLY* WANTS

Probably one of the most time-consuming aspects of your business at first will be figuring out exactly what the client wants. Unfortunately, there are no standard names for the various ways in which dogs are groomed. Your client may come to you from another part of the country and request a particular clip by name. You will be wise to be sure that both you and the client are discussing the same style. A good example of this breakdown in communication is the "Puppy Clip" for Poodles. The American Kennel Club recognizes only one style as a "Puppy Clip" when referring to the grooming done on Poodles for the show ring. This is completely described in the official standard for the Poodle breed. Many dog groomers around the country have never read that official standard and invent some sort of simple clip that they tag as a "puppy clip." Most of your clients are not even aware that there is an official standard, let alone any official description of the particular clip. When in doubt, ask what the client means.

Asking the client can sometimes be a frustrating experience. If you are less than tactful, the client is likely to think that you know very little. After all, his last groomer knew exactly what he meant when he asked for this clip. You must understand that your client is so totally uninformed that he has no way to judge how much a groomer knows about his trade. If his dog comes home looking nice, clean, neat and free of external parasites, then the groomer did a good job. If this client has only seen the work of one groomer, he is almost certain to believe that he has seen "correct" work. You are not likely to convince the client that the first groomer wasn't much good at his work, but you can, if you are careful, convince him that every groomer is an individual and that all do somewhat different work.

Frequently, the client will take offense at your attempts to clarify his wishes unless your questions are very carefully phrased. The client does not understand or care that there is no standardization among dog groomers. His only interest is in his own dog and in having that dog groomed in the manner to which he has become accustomed. The client is inclined to take your questions as either doubt or criticism on your part. He does not grasp the fact that the only way you will be able to find out how he wants his dog to look is to ask. The client thinks you are questioning his ability to explain what he wants to have done. Sometimes, of course, it will be possible for you to have a fair idea of what is wanted simply by the way the dog looks. If it has not been too long since the dog was groomed previously, you will still be able to tell what sort of pattern had been done. If this is the case, you can simply confirm through your questions what your eyes tell you has been done. A nice tactful way to determine length, for instance, is to say something like "Did you want that fairly short, so you won't have to do too much upkeep at home?" Notice that you have let the customer assume that you know exactly the style, all you are asking about is length. "Did your other groomer usually. . ." is another good lead-in for a question. Again, this allows the client the comfort of believing that you know basically what he wants, but in the intricacies of your profession there are some little variations you want to be sure about before doing the work. Your client will usually be more than willing to accept that there are some minor things that might differ.

Another way to approach the question of what the client wants is a simple, honest disclaimer: "I don't believe that I am familiar with that clip by that particular name. Perhaps I know it by some other name, could you describe it to me?" This can be tolerated well by the client, and if presented pleasantly can work. If on the other hand the groomer sounds even slightly condescending when using this sort of approach, the client may be offended.

The entire time that you are listening to the client describe what he wants to have done with his dog, you are going to be sure to make notes. Writing notes as you go along can avoid confusion in the final analysis.

There are some visual aids that can simplify your client's decisions. These can give him a ready reference and a definite picture to point to when he really has little or no idea what he wants. These can also clarify what he is trying to describe when he does know what he wants.

One of the visual aids you might choose to use could be a book of simple clip patterns. You can assemble such a book yourself from a variety of sources if the pictures are nice and clear. If you do this, a neatly typed description below each picture might be of some help. These pictures should be basic outline-type drawings that are easy to understand. You might add a brief note in red at the top of the page to point out any special characteristics of a clip. You would want to note if a particular clip is very short or if it requires a lot of brushing at home.

You can always use one of the many fine books of grooming patterns on the market, but you may find that the client has so many choices in a book of this nature that it is difficult for him to reach a decision. Upon occasion, a client looking at an entire book of this nature may try to start combining various features from several patterns with either disastrous or ludicrous results. This is especially true of those folks who have Poodles or a breed that might be clipped to resemble a Poodle.

One very practical way to use the excellent line drawings found in some dog-grooming books is to make photocopies of selected pages that you can then assemble into an attractive notebook. This allows you to choose a limited number of variations that will have the effect of making your client able to make a choice more easily. In the case of breeds in which there is basically only one style of grooming, you will of course need only one picture. Be sure that these are specifically marked. Try to understand that your client will not readily see and recognize the difference between two similar styles. This is especially true of some of the terrier breeds. The differences may be slight, and the client may not see them at all unless they are pointed out.

Wall charts are available that show many different grooming styles for Poodles as well as basic styles for all other breeds. These are nice and colorful, but can often confuse the novice owner. The pictures on these charts are attractive but not necessarily very descriptive. If you have some of the charts, you might wish to have them framed as part of the decor in your waiting area. The client will be able to see them easily and can take his time making up his mind before trying to tell you what he likes.

Still another way to make up a selection of pictures for your client to use as a guide is to use snapshots of various dogs that have been groomed by you or in your establishment. Whether they have been done recently or in a place you had worked previously is of little importance. These pictures will have the added advantage of showing some examples of your work. A major disadvantage to the snapshot album is that snapshots can be misleading—the client may not be able to get a good idea of the style.

One very nice way to help your clients in choosing a pattern for their pets is to combine the snapshots with line drawings in your album. In this way, the client is given a very accurate drawing of the way the clip is shaped on the dog while the snapshot conveys better how this pattern looks on a real animal.

11

Handle with Caution . . .

The Difficult Dog

IN YOUR PRACTICE of dog grooming you will often find that Man's Best Friend is not necessarily enamored of his groomer. It is not uncommon to find that some of the dogs brought to you for grooming will be less than pleased to have a new hairdo and will express their displeasure by biting. Some will simply nip or threaten, some will bite viciously and with very little provocation.

Because you have already learned to groom dogs, no doubt you are more than well aware that not everything you will be called upon to do is pleasant, and some things can be downright painful to the dog. Cutting toenails can be very uncomfortable for the dog, especially if the nails have been left unattended for a long time. Mats hurt when combed out, infected ears are already painful and, while cleaning is necessary, it doesn't feel good at all. Ticks and burrs can make sores as can many other foreign objects that get into the coat.

The normal course of grooming can be quite uncomfortable and a trial for the dog especially if he has not been well cared for and you should be able to understand that the dog might easily resent the apparent cause of his discomfort—you. The dog of course has no way to understand that it is his neglectful owner who is actually at fault. The fact that you understand the situation does not render you any more willing to be bitten and that is what a major portion of this chapter is all about. It is important to your business that you be able to use your hands, not have them bandaged. But it is also important that the dog survive the grooming experience intact.

PROTECTING YOURSELF FROM INJURY

Naturally, you are concerned with protecting yourself from being bitten or severely scratched while grooming dogs. In your career, it is almost inevitable that at some time you will definitely risk being bitten, but if you are wise, you will minimize this risk as much as possible. It is not necessary to be excessively rough with the dog in order to protect yourself. In many cases, you will be able to minimize time and discomfort to the dog through the use of the same measures that will protect you as well.

Stop-Look-Listen

One of the first clues you will get that a dog is more than usually likely to bite may be the owner's phrase, "He has never bitten anyone in his life." Especially when this remark is offered with no preamble and is not in answer to an inquiry, take heed. Why did the owner need to make this remark if the dog in fact has never bitten anyone? Owners don't like to think their dogs would ever do any harm (the exception is the so-called family "guard" dog, in which case the owner might be proud of vicious behavior), and most owners are reluctant to admit that their pet is really a nasty-tempered little beast.

Another warning signal given by owners is the story told about how they are bringing their pet to you for grooming because "such and such salon mistreated him so." If you are on good terms with the owners or groomers at such and such salon, you might wait until the owner leaves and give them a call. Sometimes you will be surprised to hear what the situation really is. Clients do not seem to be aware that groomers, like any group of professional people, are acquainted with each other and that they do share information.

Yet another tipoff phrase is "He just won't let me brush him." Especially when the subject dog is a little guy of only a few pounds, exactly what does "he won't let me" mean? It could mean that he bites the owner and you can be reasonably sure that if the dog bites his owner he will at least make an effort to bite you if you persist in trying to brush him.

Other key phrases are: "He is a little feisty," "He is kind of fussy about his feet" (or his ears or tummy or face or whatever), "He just hates going to the groomer" or variations on these themes. Learn to listen to the owner and to understand what is really meant. Listen ·

between the lines. Sometimes you can lead the owner into actually telling you that the dog might bite. Ask what it is the little fellow does when he "won't let you brush him." The owner isn't likely to admit that his beloved pet bites, but he might tell you that the dog "sort of snaps" at him, which is just another way to say bites.

Well informed is well prepared. Try to learn as much as you can about the dog when you first meet the dog and owner. The first things that you learn are likely to be things the owner tells you through his remarks. The next clues that you get will probably come from the dog himself. Learn to watch the dog's behavior. If the dog ducks away from your hand with a rather jerky motion, watch out. If the dog bolts to the far end of the leash when you approach and strains to stay as far from you as possible, be careful. This dog could be a fear biter and as such could be dangerously prone to biting. The dog who bites from fear is especially dangerous because he truly believes that he is fighting for his life (in extreme cases) and he may fight with the strength born of desperation. Even a very small dog can deliver a painful bite and some of the bigger dogs can bite hard enough to cripple. In the case of the small dog in the owner's arms, be careful when removing the dog who is scrambling to get away as the owner chants "It's O.K., Good Boy, it's O.K." Good Boy may take a quick nip if given the chance. Be especially careful of the dog who squirms and wiggles in his efforts to escape and who is turned loose by the owner. The owner may well have been bitten previously and doesn't intend to have it happen again. One reason that owners are reluctant to tell you that their dog will bite is that they are embarrassed. They may also be afraid that you will refuse to groom the dog if you are told that the dog will bite.

Upon occasion, an owner will come right out and tell you that his dog is a biter. Always be sure to thank the owner for this information and accept it in a noncritical way. It took courage for the owner to make this admission to you. You might ask if there are special circumstances that might provoke biting. In some instances, forewarned is all that it takes to be able to avoid a bite entirely. Firmness and caution with a dog of this type can often avoid any confrontation at all.

If your grooming experience has been confined to your own dogs, it can be quite an unnerving experience to have a dog make a serious effort at inflicting a real bite to some part of your anatomy. It is extremely important that you be well prepared for this mentally. If you are not, you will tend to be hesitant in your handling of the dog who has made the attempt and may ultimately be unable to groom the dog at all if you shy away from his efforts to bite.

The best protection that you can have against dog bites is experience. The more experience that you have in handling dogs in general, the less likely you are to be bitten simply because you will have learned to read the behavior and can avoid a bite. "Dogs" doesn't mean just your own dogs, but as many different dogs of different breeds and different temperaments as possible. While there is no substitute for experience (and no real shortcut either) there are some protective measures you can plan for in advance.

Muzzles

Muzzles can be a great asset to any dog groomer. This does not refer to the commercially sold muzzles, however. These muzzles are generally too bulky and awkward to facilitate grooming. For the most part commercial muzzles are designed to keep the dog comfortable while the muzzle is in place because they are meant to be worn for a fairly long period of time. Your interest is primarily in controlling the dog effectively and safely and to avoid being bitten. You have no wish to keep the muzzle in place for any extended period of time. This can most easily be accomplished by muzzling the dog only at its first attempt to bite. By muzzling, you will be able to do the job at hand more quickly and thus render the amount of discomfort for the dog less than if the procedure were prolonged.

One of the best muzzles for this purpose is the type commonly called a *gauze muzzle* or an *emergency muzzle*. A length of gauze (or soft nylon rope) is wrapped under the muzzle of the dog and tied once on top, brought back under and tied once underneath. The ends of the gauze (or rope) are then drawn behind the dog's ears and secured with a bow or slip knot. With practice, this can be accomplished quickly and easily even with a dog who is vigorously protesting the entire operation. (You might want to practice this a few times with one of your own dogs if you have never done it before.) The muzzle should be tied snugly. With this muzzle in place and the dog correctly attached to the grooming arm, it should be possible to cut toenails or perform other needed work without fear of a bite.

In the case of the extremely short-nosed breeds, the gauze muzzle will not work because the length of the dog's face is so short that there is no place to wrap the gauze. It is possible to fabricate a muzzle that is quite effective and safe for the short-nosed breeds. Because many of these breeds also have protruding eyes that are subject to injury, it is desirable to protect the eyes of the dog at the same time that you are protecting yourself from being bitten. To achieve both of these objectives, you may wish to make a muzzle from a rigid plastic cup. To do this, first punch a series of holes in the bottom and sides of the cup. This can be accomplished with a nail (if the nail is heated red hot it will make smooth holes), or with a punch. Next punch four holes evenly spaced around the rim of the cup. Into each of the four holes around the rim secure a heavy shoelace. The size of these cups can vary and you might wish to make several of these muzzles in different sizes. The less the cup tapers from top to bottom, the more effective it will be, and will be more comfortable for the dog. The mouth of the cup should be wide enough to fit over the entire face of the short-nosed breeds so that the eyes are covered. Now tie the shoelaces at the back to the dog's head in this manner: one shoelace goes over the ear and one shoelace goes under the ear on each side, and all four are fastened with a bow knot or a slip knot at the back of the dog's head.

Do not leave this type of muzzle in place for an extended period of time. Even with lots of holes in the bottom and sides of the cup, the air supply is lessened and the dog could become overheated and thus be injured. This muzzle should only be used in extreme situations because the very flat-faced dogs tend to become overheated easily and can become dangerously overheated in a very short time, but this muzzle will protect the eyes from injury if the dog thrashes around. Some of the short-faced breeds have eyes so protruding that even a very slight blow to the eye can cause serious damage and even loss of the eye.

The Grooming Arm and Noose

Presumably you are accustomed to using a grooming arm and noose on your grooming table. If you are not in the habit of using the arm and noose, think seriously about the value of this piece of equipment. The grooming arm should be adjustable so that you can use it with almost any size dog. The sort of grooming arms that are sold commercially come in several lengths—choose the longest available. When choosing a grooming arm, be sure to select one of the better grades because some of the less expensive models are quite flimsy and will not stand up to hard use. In selecting an arm, you will have to decide whether to use one that is permanently mounted through a hole drilled in the grooming table, or a clamp-on model. Each has its advantages. The first of course is very stable and draws strength from being securely mounted. The second type has more versatility. Either kind can work well and you will know best what will suit your own needs.

When securing a dog on the table, the noose, which is attached to the grooming arm, can be placed around the neck of the dog and the arm can be adjusted to a height that will allow the dog to stand comfortably or to sit, but that will prevent him from lying down or jumping off the table. If the arm is positioned at the end of the table, the dog is less likely to turn around. If the arm is placed in the center of one side of the table, the dog can be turned from side to side so that you are able to groom both sides without moving around the table. If you are working on an especially fidgety dog, you might wish to use two grooming arms. One noose then secures the head of the dog and the other arm and noose can control the rear. The second arm is clamped on the table in the center of one side, the noose is placed around the loin area of the dog and the arm is raised to a height that prevents the dog from sitting but that will allow him to stand comfortably. Now the dog must stand and he cannot turn around. This is a safe and effective way to maintain control over the dog and to protect yourself from being bitten.

Another piece of equipment that can be used in conjunction with the grooming arm is an item called a *sling,* which holds the entire dog off the table. Essentially, this is a canvas bag with holes that allow the dog's legs to protrude. The sling allows the groomer to work on the feet of the dog, yet prevents the dog from reaching the groomer to bite. The major disadvantage in the use of the sling is that the groomer is not allowed easy access to the body of the dog.

Kennel Leads

One effective way to control a snappish dog when it arrives for grooming is the use of a *kennel lead.* This is a simple piece of equipment formed from a length of material (flat nylon webbing, flat cotton webbing, lightweight nylon rope) with a ring on one end that allows the rope or webbing to be passed through, thus forming a leash and collar all in one. The advantage in this is that one size fits all and the collar will tighten if the dog attempts to pull away. It also

163

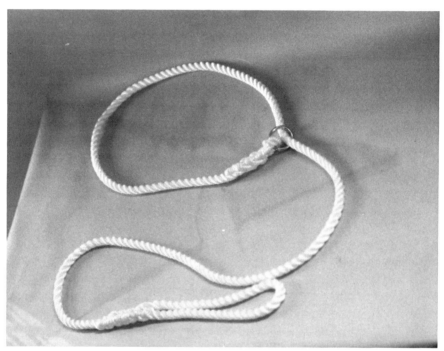

This simple nylon kennel lead acts as both collar and leash and allows the groomer to restrain and control larger dogs, or dogs that bite.

allows you to flip the loop over the head of the dog without placing your hands dangerously near the animal's mouth. The dog can then be led or controlled as needed.

A kennel lead should always be used on a large dog. If the dog arrives with a regular flat collar, chances are he can pull back and slip out of that collar if he is really determined, and then you are faced with the prospect of catching a possibly hostile dog. If you use a kennel lead routinely, you will seldom have this problem. A kennel lead also will allow you to hold a biting dog away from your body if need be.

Catch Noose

Every kennel or grooming shop should have a *catch noose* available for emergency use. There are many catch nooses available commercially, but there is no real need for the average groomer to go to the expense of purchasing such an item when it is easy to make a very acceptable noose at a very low cost.

A catch noose is a piece of equipment designed to allow the individual to slip a noose over the head of an animal without bringing any part of his own anatomy within biting or clawing distance. A very simple catch noose can be made from a length of 1/2- or 3/4-inch-diameter plastic water pipe and a piece of very heavy-duty rubber-coated electrical wire. Using a piece of the plastic pipe approximately 2½ to 3 feet in length and a piece of the electrical wire about four times as long as the pipe, simply double the electrical wire and feed it through the length of pipe so that a loop protrudes from one end of the pipe and the two loose ends of the wire protrude from the other end. This allows the groomer to slip the loop over the head of a would-be biter and pull the free ends of the wire until the loop is snug around the dog's neck. The dog is secured so that he cannot bite and yet can be gently and safely maneuvered into or out of a crate, or off or onto a table. This catch noose is especially convenient when a dog already in a crate shows that he has no intention whatsoever of coming out, or if a dog gets loose in the grooming shop and threatens to bite when an attempt is made to catch him. Some dogs feel threatened when placed in a situation from which they cannot back away, such as in a crate, or when they feel cornered, and will bite under these circumstances. The use of the catch noose allows the dog to be gently but firmly secured with a minimum of fuss or bother. The less alarmed the dog is, the less likely he is to bite. The catch noose also gives the groomer a comforting sense of being in control of the situation and of being in no personal danger from a bite. For this reason the groomer is able to handle the dog in a calm fashion that will further reassure the dog and render it even less likely to bite. Most owners might recoil from the very idea of using an implement such as a catch noose and, indeed, some groomers are reluctant to use this tool. Do not allow your prejudices to deprive you of this very useful piece of equipment. Not only is the catch noose a safety measure for the groomer, it can also be of great value to the peace of mind of both dog and groomer.

PROTECTING THE DOG FROM INJURY

In dealing with the really difficult dog, one of the foremost considerations of the groomer must be the protection of the dog itself. While the groomer must protect himself, it must never be done by risking injury to the dogs in his care.

Odd as it may sound, oftentimes the same measures that protect the groomer will also protect the dog. This is especially true of the catch noose. This very humane instrument can allow control of a frightened or biting dog while keeping the animal as safe as possible. If you are unsure of the use of the catch noose, practice on your own dogs until you are able to handle the noose in a calm and effective manner. In using the catch noose, the dog should be allowed to keep its feet securely on the floor so that it is not being choked. The length of the handle protects the groomer from any attempt at biting and the dog is kept safely away from the object of his fear—the groomer. By your maintaining a calm and gentle manner, many dogs that might otherwise be so hysterical as to prevent grooming entirely can successfully be groomed.

The use of the cup muzzle, as was described earlier, can also protect the dog from injury should he thrash around and inflict possible injury to his eyes or head in his efforts to escape. Having the muzzle securely in place seems somehow to reassure some dogs. Use of the muzzle can further protect the dog from a prolonged struggle that might cause the animal to become overheated. Through the use of the muzzle, the groomer is allowed to quickly accomplish some tasks that might take much longer if every effort was met with an attempt at biting.

Surprisingly enough, very few dogs seem to hold any sort of grudge. Even though the groomer has had to muzzle the dog in order to avoid a bite (while doing the toenails for instance), once the job has been done and the muzzle has been removed, the dog will seldom make an effort to take any revenge. Some extremely difficult dogs will make an attempt to throw themselves off the table in their efforts to avoid the attentions of the groomer. This is an instance in which the use of the grooming sling or the double grooming arm can help avoid injury to the dog and facilitate grooming as well. It is possible to prevent the dog from throwing himself off the table without the use of either of these measures, but it can greatly slow down the work being done.

Sometimes it will pay the groomer to make a few simple efforts to reassure the dog that all is well and that he is not going to be hurt. In the case of dogs that have never been groomed before, the sound of the clippers can provoke instant panic with its attendant dangers to both dog and groomer. This is especially true if the groomer turns the clippers on and begins work immediately. Often simply turning the clippers on and allowing the dog to hear the sound without feeling the accompanying vibrations will be enough to allow the dog to relax and accept clipping with a minimum of fuss. The less fuss the dog puts up, the less likely it is that he will cause injury to himself or to the groomer. Another way to further avoid panic is to begin the clipping at the rear of the dog rather than on the face or head.

Physical Problems

In the category of really difficult dogs, you might wish to consider also the dog who is not necessarily a vicious animal, but one that has physical problems that might make grooming a hazard to the dog himself. This might include the dog that has a bad heart or a bad back or some other physical handicap. If, in addition to the physical problem, the dog is also nervous or frightened, he could easily cause serious injury to himself.

It is always wise to ask the owner of a new dog coming to your shop whether the dog has any special problems. This would of course normally be done when filling out the regular record card for a new client. Be especially careful to inquire about physical limitations if the dog is of an extreme age or if it appears to be lame, blind or crippled in some manner. Owners often forget to mention problems because they are so accustomed to the dog that they tend to forget that the problem exists. The owner seldom realizes that grooming can be a stressful situation for the dog even if it is only the stress of being away from home. This stress is compounded if the dog is not groomed regularly and must have some uncomfortable services performed.

Hyperactives

There are some dogs who are so extremely hyperactive that they pose a risk for themselves in any unusual situation. Some of these dogs can be handled through firmness coupled with gentleness. (The best recommendation that you can make to the owner of a hyperactive dog is that the dog be enrolled in an obedience class where the dog can learn self-control. Naturally, this would not apply if the dog is of an extreme age or has physical handicaps.) Too often, these hyperactive dogs are as much a product of their owners as of their own tendency toward hyperactivity. The owner simply accepts the over-active behavior and makes excuses for it rather than pursue the time-consuming task of teaching the dog more acceptable behavior. If this is the case, the dog may respond well to your firmness.

The major danger for the hyperactive dog is that he will so excite himself that there is a real possibility he will become dangerously overheated. Overheating can kill, and if the dog is so totally out of control that he is becoming overheated, your best move is simply to place the dog in a wire crate for maximum ventilation and perhaps turn a fan on the animal or spray him lightly with plain water. If the dog does not calm down and relax he could actually be the cause of his own death. One way to spot these potential problem dogs is to watch the dog's behavior when he is first brought into your shop. Is the dog a veritable whirling dervish? Is he literally foaming in his excitement? Is he panting and straining at the leash? Sometimes a tactful remark to the owner about how excited the dog is will elicit the information that the dog is always like this. This can be the warning you need.

When hyperactivity is combined with a heart problem, the situation is doubly hazardous. Another potentially dangerous situation is the hyperactive dog who is also overweight, because the overweight condition and the hyperactivity both place an excessive strain on the heart.

None of this is meant to imply that the physically handicapped dog does not need to be groomed. Quite the contrary. Not only is it important for the dog with medical problems to be kept well groomed for appearance's sake, it is also important that he be kept clean for the sake of his health and well-being. Keeping the skin and coat clean and clipped to a comfortable length can be of benefit to the handicapped dog's general health and welfare. Regular grooming helps keep the dog free from the stress of external parasites, keeps his skin in good condition and free of irritation and avoids the stress of a difficult grooming that might result if the coat were allowed to become excessively dirty and matted.

To best serve the needs of those dogs with physical problems, try to arrange for a neat short style that will subject the dog to a minimum of stress during the grooming itself. Keep the combing of mats to a minimum. Try to make all the grooming procedures as stress-free as possible. In the case of extremely obese or hyperactive dogs, use a cooler than normal setting when drying the dog so that he does not become overheated. In the event that the dog becomes excited and struggles or fights to the point that he appears to be in distress, place the dog in a crate for a while until he becomes more calm.

If you find something out of the ordinary that seems to indicate some sort of handicap, old injury or bone or joint problem, take the time to stop your work and call the owner. It is far better to find out what the problem might be than to continue with the grooming and risk a possible injury to the dog. In some cases, you may discover that the owner is not aware that the problem exists and that he will be most grateful that you have alerted him to a potentially hazardous condition. This is especially true if the dog was acquired recently.

Upon occasion you may discover that a dog in your care has a condition that is so serious that to continue grooming could risk the dog's life. Fortunately this is rare, but it can happen. If you should discover something you feel to be life threatening, call the owner. Do not proceed with the grooming until you have discussed the situation with the owner.

Real Emergencies

Virtually every groomer has had the heart-stopping experience of having a dog that has a true life-threatening emergency in the shop. This could be an old dog who collapses with heart failure or the animal that goes into shock from a previously unknown allergy to a medicated soap or dip. In the event that such an emergency occurs, naturally your first action will be to render the appropriate first aid and then to rush the animal to a veterinarian. It is to be hoped that, as a groomer, you will be on such terms with your veterinarian that you can expect him to render first aid to your client dogs. If you do not have such a veterinarian, by all means try to locate a doctor who will act as your "on call" veterinarian.

In a life or death situation, wait to call the owner until emergency first aid has been given and the dog is in the hands of the veterinarian. Then you should call the owner and explain the situation.

First Aid

Every dog groomer should be well versed in canine first aid. This is important for many reasons. A thorough knowledge of first aid will be of great value to the groomer in discovering potential problems as well as in rendering emergency help to a dog before rushing him to the veterinary clinic. A thorough knowledge of first aid will also help the groomer to know when medical help is not indicated. There are many fine books that deal exclusively with first aid for dogs. By all means, be more than just passingly familiar with basic first aid procedures. Keep a first aid chart or book close at hand for easy referral in an emergency situation.

A first aid kit should certainly be a part of any grooming salon. You can assemble such a kit for yourself and maintain it in a handy location. A good comprehensive first aid book will usually give suggestions regarding the contents that should be included in your first aid kit. Do check with your own veterinarian and ask him what he recommends. Here again, a close working relationship with your veterinarian is invaluable. Most veterinarians are more than willing to give advice about first aid. Don't, however, think that you can wait until such time as an emergency has already occurred and then expect the doctor to talk you through first aid procedures.

Sending a Sick Dog Home

It is to be hoped that this situation will be noticed before the owner has left the dog with you for grooming. It is much easier to refuse to even begin work than it is to have to call the owner to let him know that for one reason or another you are not able to groom his dog. The exception to this rule is the dog that is discovered to have some sort of serious and previously unknown medical problem. Then the owner is generally pleased that you have cared enough to call and suggest immediate treatment for the dog.

Whether or not you complete the grooming work on a dog with a previously undiscovered medical problem is strictly up to you. You may feel that the grooming will help make further treatment easier and if this is the case, and you are sure that you will be able to complete your work without hazard to the dog, then go ahead. If you have any question that the continuation of your work will be of benefit to the dog, or if you feel that the dog is in any danger whatsoever, then call the owner immediately. Tact is necessary both to avoid insulting the client and to avoid alarming him. It is tactful to imply that the owner was unaware of the problem and thus avoid putting him on the defensive. Owners tend to feel that they are being accused of neglecting their pets if something is wrong. It is often easiest to make the client feel comfortable with a phrase like, "I was sure that you would want to know . . ." and then continue with a brief description of the problem. Sometimes the owner will seem unsure of the reason for your call. If that is the case you may have to be a bit more specific. You might say, "I thought I should let you know about this so that you could pick up your dog and take her to the doctor. We can complete her grooming next week after she has had a chance to have this taken care of."

Keep in mind that the owner is going to be furious if you present him with a dripping wet dog. If you have gotten as far as the bathtub in grooming the dog, at least try to get the animal as dry as possible. (If the dog has collapsed or is in some other apparently life-threatening situation, of course you will not wait to get him dry.) If you feel that the dog will not be placed in any further danger, you may wish to wait until the drying is almost complete and then call the owner.

Some owners will try to get you to prescribe treatment in order to avoid the cost of a veterinary visit. Even if you know what the problem is and are reasonably sure of the treatment, do not prescribe any treatment at all. You are not a veterinarian and you simply cannot afford to act in that capacity. There are far too many legal ramifications involved. Not the least of these could be a charge of practicing medicine without a license. Even if you have had to render some sort of first aid to the dog, do not tell the owner what further measures to take and do be sure that you let the owner know exactly what first aid was given (in writing is best), as well as giving a complete description of the symptoms so that the veterinarian can be informed.

Refusing To Accept the Sick or Injured Dog

If you notice a medical problem when the dog is first brought in, you should certainly call this to the attention of the owner (no matter how minor the problem appears to be) before you accept the dog for grooming. If the problem appears to be severe or you feel that grooming at this time would not be in the best interests of the dog, then you will find it necessary to refuse to accept the dog. Great tact must be exercised to avoid angering or upsetting the owner. This is especially true if this is a new client. If you have a good working relationship with your regular clients, you will probably not have any problem in sending one of their dogs home for medical reasons. Your regular customers will realize that you have only the best interests of the dog at heart. New customers may not be aware that your concern is for the dog. It will take gentle and tactful reasoning to make the owner see that you sincerely care about his dog.

For some reason, owners sometimes think that groomers simply don't want to groom their pets. (If the owner would stop to think, he would realize that without work to do groomers would have no business at all.) Many owners will act as if you are picking on them, and a gentle tone and nonjudgmental attitude are a must. Again, it is a good policy to act as if the owner had no idea that the problem existed at all. In fact, the owner may be totally unaware of the situation and will feel very guilty that he hasn't noticed the problem. On the other hand, the owner may be well aware of the situation, but he still hopes that you will think he is taken quite by surprise.

One way to make the owner more comfortable is to sympathize with both him and his dog. Never, never indicate that you think the owner has been neglectful. You might say something like, "Goodness, that leg really seems to be bothering him, doesn't it?" Then, after further examination, "No wonder! Look here, he has cut himself. That is really a difficult spot to see, too. I'm afraid to go ahead and groom him with such a deep cut. Would you like to call your vet from here and take him over? I can reschedule his grooming for . . ." To help keep the client and to reassure him that you really are interested in his dog, always make the offer of a specific day to reschedule the dog's appointment.

If for some reason you feel that the dog is so ill that you will not be able to groom him at all, either today or in the future (perhaps an animal with a severe heart or respiratory problem) you can be most tactful by suggesting that the owner call you back to reschedule a grooming after the dog is well stabilized on medication.

There is, of course, yet another situation that will arise from time to time, and that is the problem of the old dog who could expire at any time from his various problems, but that still needs to be groomed. If you simply are not willing to risk having the dog choose your place of business in which to die, you will have to refuse the dog. It is very difficult to be tactful enough to avoid offending the owner, but you must at least try not to give offense. After all, this owner may acquire a new dog after the demise of the current pet. One alternative suggestion might be that the veterinary clinic could perhaps groom the dog and a doctor would be on hand if the need arose. If you are convinced that the owner is aware of the condition of his dog and is able to accept the fact that his pet could die at any time, it is probably better for you (in a business sense) to simply do your best for the dog. Do keep the grooming experience as nonstressful as possible and be sure that the dog is as comfortable and as relaxed as possible. In the case of this type of dog, call the owner at any sign of a problem. Face it, the odds are in your favor. What percentage of his time does the dog actually spend in your place of business?

REFUSING THE VICIOUS DOG

When faced with a really vicious dog, you will have to make your own determination as to the amount of risk you are able and willing to take. Remembering always that forewarned is forearmed, you may be willing to take on dogs that are extremely difficult and count on your own abilities to avoid injury to your person. In some cases, just your confidence will allow you to groom a dog that another groomer may be unable to handle.

It is virtually inevitable that at some time during your career as a groomer you will face a dog you consider too vicious to take the risk of grooming. The problem becomes that of refusing this dog in a tactful manner.

Some owners are simply not able to accept the fact that their pet

173

is not a nice dog. Not only is this kind of dog not nice, he is downright dangerous, and the owner often cannot come to grips with this situation. In the eyes of the owner, you are obviously just not competent to handle a "feisty" dog. Don't let the owner project this image on you. If you are not willing to risk working with the dog in question, that is your right, There is no law requiring that you place yourself in jeopardy in order to satisfy the customer. A kind manner and a pleasant voice may help to take the sting out of the fact that you are just not willing to groom this untrustworthy dog.

It is to be hoped that the dog has shown his true colors when he was first brought in. When this is the case, it is fairly easy simply to refuse to even start on the grooming. If the dog has made a determined effort to bite while the owner is still present, there is little that the owner can actually blame you for having done. At the very worst, the client might try to tell you how to approach the dog or he might feel that you have "frightened" the animal. Be prepared, the client is almost certain to be offended. The more kind and gentle you can appear, the better. One way to handle this situation is to say something that makes the owner feel that your first thought is for the dog. This might be something like, "He really seems upset. You know, I don't think that we can groom him without upsetting him even more and I really don't want to do that." Another way to put this is, "Has he always acted this way at the groomer? Have you ever considered that perhaps it would be better for him if you did his grooming at home so that he won't be so distressed?"

A few owners will just simply not take the hint and you may have to be more blunt. Even if this is necessary, good manners must still prevail. If you must be completely forthright, try something along these lines, "I'm afraid that we are going to have to refuse to groom Poopsie. We just don't deal with dogs that bite. I'm sorry." If you know of a groomer in the area who is particularly good at handling tough dogs, this is the time to recommend that groomer. You might even offer to give the groomer a call and make an appointment for this dog. The conversation might begin this way, "You know, Mrs. Dog Owner is very good with difficult dogs. Would you like me to call her and see if she can groom your dog for you?" You may find that this dog has already been turned away by the only groomer in town who deals with the really tough dogs, or even that the dog has been going there and has finally become too much. In any event, you have at least been polite, you have attempted to help the owner out and you have made every effort to make a bad situation as pleasant as possible.

It is more difficult to call an owner and have him come to pick up his vicious dog after you have already accepted it for grooming. In this situation, you are wide open for blame and you really have little defense except your own good reputation. Some dogs will seem to be just fine in the presence of the owner and then show their real personality once the owner has gone. Naturally, you will do all you can to calm the dog, but if nothing works and you are unwilling to take the risks involved, by all means call the owner to come and pick up his pet. Customer relations are certainly important, but not so important that you must take unnecessary risks. One way to minimize the client's displeasure is to make the problem appear to be one of devotion to the owner: "Little Ralph just went crazy when you left. He started fighting and trying to bite. He must be just a one-person dog. I'm afraid that he is going to hurt himself trying to get away. Please come pick him up so that he won't be in such a frenzy." (If you are going to have to put the dog in a crate while waiting for the owner to arrive, be sure that Ralph is wearing a kennel lead so that you will be able to get him out of the crate without a fight.) This flatters the owner and makes him more likely to feel sympathetic with the dog than angry at you. The owner is not going to be pleased and you must understand his position. He was counting on having the dog groomed today and now he has to go to the trouble of finding another groomer, making another appointment and taking the dog to yet another shop. You are not likely to fare well in later descriptions. You may be described as having "mistreated little Ralph," or as being too rough or any number of other and even less flattering characterizations. If your customers are generally pleased with your work, this kind of comment once in a while is not going to damage either your business or your reputation.

USING TRANQUILIZERS

The best possible advice about the use of tranquilizers is: Don't. The use of tranquilizers of any kind is best left to the veterinarian. There are far too many ways for medications to react for a groomer to even consider their use in a grooming business. Not only can the tranquilizer itself pose a risk for the dog, but certain drugs must not be used in conjunction with certain insecticides (such as medicated shampoos or flea-and-tick dips), and could be fatal if used carelessly.

If you are grooming in a veterinary hospital and the doctor chooses to use a tranquilizer, then you are left in the clear insofar as responsibility is concerned. The doctor will tell you whether or not to use any medicated shampoo and whether or not the dog should be dipped for parasites. If any problem arises you will have immediate medical help at hand. Under these circumstances, you are freed from the decisions with regard to the use of tranquilizers.

Owners will sometimes ask whether you will groom a difficult dog if they take it to their veterinarian and have it tranquilized. This is a decision you should weigh carefully. Before agreeing to do the grooming, you might be well advised to call the veterinarian who would be administering the drug and ask him for his opinion. He should be able to tell you what to expect and whether the dog is at any particular risk. Be sure to ask the doctor whether it will be hazardous to use a flea-and-tick dip or a medicated shampoo.

One thing to remember is that tranquilizers are just that— tranquilizers. The drug may make the dog more calm, but it is not guaranteed to make it possible to groom a vicious animal. A dog who has been given a tranquilizer may seem quiet and relaxed, but he may still whirl into action when you make an attempt to groom him.

For some reason, groomers have the reputation of using tranquilizers for their work. By far the majority do not. Possibly this reputation has arisen from a general lack of knowledge on the part of the public. Most people have no idea at all how you go about achieving your results. They simply cannot imagine how you are able to make the dog stand still to be groomed. In another age, groomers might have been accused of witchcraft, in our more technical society, drugs seem to fit the bill. This is an explanation many uninformed owners are able to accept far more readily than the actual explanation of your abilities.

12

Of Course We Can . . .
Extra Services

IT IS INEVITABLE that you will be asked about some
services that are not precisely dog grooming but that are more or less
related to grooming. You are already familiar with the fact that you
are going to be asked many questions about things that pertain to
dogs and you are also aware that you will tend to become a point of
reference for those people who are seeking a new puppy or who want
stud service for their female.

The services that will be discussed in this chapter are more
directly related to your own business than some of the other things
that have been mentioned previously. These arc the extras that you
may or may not elect to offer to your clientele. You must weigh the
merits of these services and decide which of these would fit in well
with your particular business style and for your clientele.

PICKUP AND DELIVERY

Depending upon the area in which your grooming business is
located, pickup and delivery of dogs who are coming in for your
services might prove an extremely lucrative addition to your services
or it could prove to be far more trouble than it is worth.

No doubt many of your clients would be very pleased if you
offered a pickup and delivery service. This is especially true if you
are able to offer this service at no additional charge to the client.
Economic considerations will probably make it necessary for you to

177

make a charge for this service, however. Whether you choose to make this a direct charge to the client who takes advantage of the service or whether you elect to simply increase the overall charges in your salon so that the cost is absorbed by the entire clientele is your own decision. If you choose to make this a charge based on actual use, you will have to further decide whether the charge will be a flat rate or will be based on distance. You may find that a flat rate is a little easier because you will not have to figure each client's rate on an individual basis.

There are several reasons why this service is a popular one with grooming-salon clients. In the case of the client who does not drive or who does not have a car readily available, pickup and delivery service frees him of the need to seek out private arrangements for transportation for the dog each time it needs to be groomed. For some customers who fit into this category, availability of this service will be the deciding factor in the choice of a regular grooming salon. For other clients it is purely a matter of convenience to have the dog picked up and delivered back home. It is easy to see some of the advantages in convenience. There is no need to find a babysitter or to get the children ready to go out somewhere. There is no need for the owner to get dressed up to go out. In fact, there is no real need to interrupt the schedule of the day's activity beyond the need to answer the door. This aspect of convenience looms large in the minds of many clients. A certain percentage of your clients will appreciate this service because the dog they own is large and rowdy and they find it difficult to handle. You may even find a certain group of people among your customers who like the snob appeal of having their pet catered to in this manner.

You can certainly understand why this service would be popular, but there is more to be considered here than the interests of your clients. There are a number of factors you will need to consider when making your decision about offering this service. These are things that will directly affect you and your business.

Vehicle

Do you have an adequate vehicle to use for a pickup and delivery service? If you drive a small sports car, where will you put the dogs being picked up? You will need to have some sort of car, van or truck that is large enough to make it possible to pick up several dogs without having to go to the salon to drop off each one before picking up the next. Ideally, you should be able to fit several crates or cages into the vehicle so that the dogs are not just running around loose. Loose dogs in a vehicle have any number of opportunities to get into trouble. Two dogs might take an instant dislike to each other while you are cruising down the highway toward your shop. A dog fight inside a car is no fun. When dogs are loose in the car, it is a real risk to open the door to get in or out or to put another dog inside. One of the dogs already in the vehicle could easily jump out and you could spend the rest of the day hoping to find it. Worse yet, a dog could leap from the car and be killed in traffic.

Whatever sort of vehicle you might choose to use for a pickup and delivery service, you must be sure that it is mechanically sound and reliable. If it is not, you could spend an entire work day stranded on the road with a broken-down vehicle, a full load of client dogs and no way to get those dogs to your place of business. You must also be sure that the vehicle you will be using has enough ventilation so that the dogs do not suffer from heat during the summer months. Air conditioning is fine when the motor is running, but dogs left in a closed vehicle for even a few minutes can become dangerously overheated if there is not adequate ventilation available.

Insurance

If you do choose to offer this service to your customers, you should consult with your insurance agent to determine exactly what kind of insurance you will need to protect yourself, your business and your employees in case of an accident or an injury to one of the dogs being transported. Laws vary from state to state so you will need to make this determination based on your place of residence. Be sure your agent understands what kind of service you will be offering. You will also need to determine whether your insurance company will require that you have a different driver's license for this type of driving. In some states you may need to have a different license (*commercial* or *commercial chauffeur*) in order for your insurance to be valid when you provide a service of this nature.

Time

A very real and important consideration you must take into account before you elect to offer this kind of service is that of time. As you know, time is very important to you in your business. You

The face of this white Poodle is stained and shaggy.

The owner cut this topknot so that his pet could "see," resulting in a problem for the groomer.

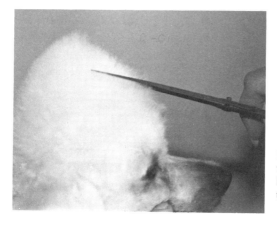

In order to blend the topknot into the area the owner has cut, it will be necessary to make the entire topknot shorter than usual.

must take into account the amount of time that will be involved in providing a service of this nature. It is all very well to save time for your clients, but you will be the one on the road for a portion of each day in order to pick up dogs and return them to their homes when their grooming is completed.

In order for you to keep your business hours as you have them set, you will want to plan to make all of your pickups before the opening hour and all of your deliveries after the hour you have set as your closing time. This can increase the length of your day by an unreasonable number of hours, especially if you have a large number of clients who wish to avail themselves of this service. One way for you to keep from working from dawn to dusk every single day is to limit the days you will provide this service to just one or two days each week. Naturally this will not please all of your clientele, but then nothing is going to please every single one of your clients.

Extra Help

If you are thinking about offering this service, you might wish to consider hiring someone to work part-time doing nothing except picking up dogs and delivering them back to their owners. This will free you to be at your place of business during your regular hours and will also allow you to do more actual grooming work. If you do choose to hire someone for this job, you will be faced with the necessity of making sure that the person you hire is licensed properly for this type of work. The licensing requirements vary from state to state, so be sure that you have checked to see what applies in your own state. When determining whether or not a candidate has the proper license and that it is current, do not be embarrassed to ask to see the license. Remember that it is your business and your vehicle and you are the one who would be liable if your employee did not have the proper sort of license. This could also cause your insurance to be invalid. You will need to be sure that your insurance coverage will be adequate to cover someone else who is employed in this position. The question of insurance of course should be taken up with your insurance agent.

Costs

In planning your expenses for a service of this kind, don't forget that you have the costs of the vehicle and its maintenance, the

181

Poodle ears should be kept clean and free of hair to help avoid ear problems.

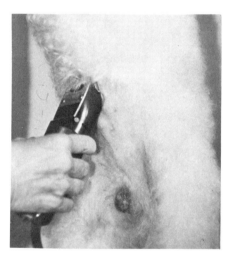

When clipping the abdomen on a male dog, it is important to exercise care not to injure the sheath.

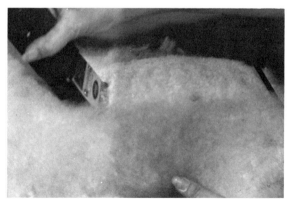

The body coat is being clipped in the direction of growth with a #5 blade.

insurance and the wages of the driver to figure in as part of the cost involved. Just because you will be doing the driving yourself doesn't mean that your time is worth nothing. Be businesslike and practical when figuring your costs. Determine about the average amount that you earn when you are grooming and use that to determine an hourly wage to be used as part of the cost for this service.

Like so many things, it is very difficult to withdraw pickup and delivery service from your clients once they have become used to this convenience. Clients enjoy being pampered and they thoroughly dislike having their special services discontinued. If you are not thinking of continuing this service indefinitely, it may be wise never to begin.

FEEDINGS

Why feedings as a special service in a grooming salon? You might be surprised at the number of your clients who genuinely believe that their dog simply cannot make it all day long without being fed. Some are sure that the dog will suffer if left unfed for even a very few hours. It is also possible that the time the dog is scheduled to be at the grooming shop is also the time during which it is normally fed at home.

You know perfectly well that it would be the unusual dog indeed that would absolutely require feeding in order to survive for the day. In fact, if a dog were in such poor condition that it had to be fed at very short intervals, it obviously would be extremely unwise to send it to the grooming salon. Nonetheless, your clients don't want to think that their dogs will go hungry.

One of the things you will need to consider when you are thinking of offering this service is the need to provide feeding dishes and a varied menu from which your clients may choose what their pets will be fed. You may be astonished at the number of varieties of dog food on the market. In order to provide a basic menu, you will probably need to stock at least two brands of each type of dog food. The types are dry food (which may be fed either dry or moistened), the soft moist products, which include all the various burgers, and finally canned foods, which can range from all-meat products to some that are nearly all cereal.

Naturally, some of your clients will wish to bring along whatever food their own pet is accustomed to eating. You will also

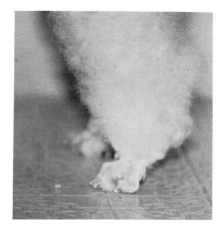

The Poodle's foot has been clipped with a #15 blade.

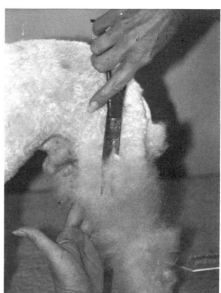

Shears are used to blend the longer hair on the leg into the short body coat.

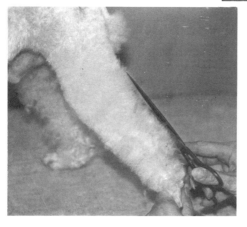

The leg is stretched straight so that the hair can be shaped with the shears. When blending the hair on the legs, cut in the direction of growth or, as shown here, directly against the direction of growth. Do not cut across the growth.

need to be ready to keep track of the amount the dog is generally fed and at what time he is used to receiving his meals.

This kind of service is a very nice touch in a really posh salon where glamour and special services are the order of the day. Depending on the area in which your shop is located and the general clientele you are serving, this service may or may not be greatly in demand.

On a practical note, although offering a midday feeding for the dogs may be very attractive for the clients, it can be a real pain for the shop owner. It becomes necessary for you to have a full set of feeding instructions for each dog as well as the grooming instructions you would normally have. You will also be faced with the added problem of food storage, providing feeding dishes, and of course those dishes will have to be washed unless you plan to purchase disposable feeding dishes, which are convenient though a bit costly. One point you should consider is that many dogs simply will not eat at all while they are away from home and thus may simply waste a serving of dog food.

Another and perhaps more important consideration is your own liability for the dogs in your care. If a dog is fed at your salon and subsequently becomes ill, you may be sure that the finger of blame is going to point in your direction whether or not there is any basis for suspecting that the food was the cause of the illness. It is sometimes astounding what the client will blame on the groomer and a dog that becomes ill after being fed at the grooming shop makes it easy for the client to fix the blame.

When weighing the pros and cons of offering this service, one other factor should be taken into consideration. Dogs who are fed need to be able to relieve themselves shortly afterward. The digestive system of the dog is relatively short and processes food quickly. If dogs are fed then they are going to have to go outdoors within a fairly short time after the meal is eaten.

If your shop is situated so that you can provide a secure area out of doors for the dogs to relieve themselves, perhaps this need not be a problem. The only inconvenience will then be the necessity to take the various dogs outdoors, allow them to relieve themselves, and of course, clean up the area afterward. Keep in mind that some dogs will have no qualms about relieving themselves in the cage in which they are kept at the grooming shop. There are few things more frustrating than to discover that the dog you have just finished

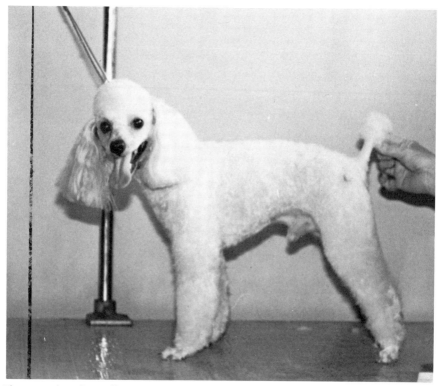

The completed Poodle sports a neat Kennel Clip that will be easy for the owner to care for. Most owners do not enjoy having to do much coat care between groomings.

grooming has soiled himself and is now going to have to have another bath. Not only is this frustrating, it is time consuming as well.

All in all, feeding is a service you should think over very carefully before committing yourself to. The major advantage to offering this service is strictly one of customer relations. The disadvantages are fairly plain to see. In figuring the cost of this service so that you may decide what to charge the client, you will be surprised to see that the cost of the food itself is very minor when compared to the time involved in feeding, cleaning and dishwashing.

Naturally, if a client brings along a snack or even a meal for his dog, you should certainly be pleasant and make every effort to accommodate the customer. From time to time you may have a client who shows up with enough food and treats to feed the dog for a week. In general, this client is one who feels guilty about leaving his poor little dog in the hands of the awful dog groomer and who puts balm on his conscience by giving the dog all kinds of special goodies. By all means, play along with the client. Never ever make fun of this kind of behavior. There is no need to cause a problem and perhaps lose a client over a situation that is really very minor. If you have very strong feelings against feeding the dog while he is at the shop, simply return the uneaten food to the owner when the dog is ready to leave and explain that the dog missed his owner so much that he just would not eat. This will satisfy the owner and speaks well for your care and concern.

EARLY ARRIVAL—LATE PICKUP

Another service that can be very much in demand is arranging for dogs to come in before the regular opening hours of the shop or arranging for them to be picked up after normal closing hours. This kind of service is popular because people have such busy lives and such odd work schedules that sometimes it is difficult for them to fit in a trip to the grooming shop during regular shop hours. People who leave for work very early in the morning will certainly appreciate being able to drop the dog off on their way to work rather than having to rush home at lunchtime or after work to get the dog and make a special trip back to the grooming salon. Other people have numerous commitments and may find it difficult to get back to the grooming shop before closing time.

Like any other special service, this is one that should be well thought out before offering it to the public. Like pickup and delivery service, this service is one to which your customers will become attached. They will like being able to drop the dog off at an early hour or being able to pick the dog up on the way home from work. Once the customer has become used to this service he is not going to be thrilled if it is discontinued.

Although this is a service that will certainly please your customers, remember that one of the reasons that you are in business for yourself is to please *you*. It is all too easy to fall into the trap of trying to please everyone and ultimately pleasing no one at all, particularly yourself. In the chapter on scheduling your time, special hours were discussed. If you have planned your schedule well, it should be such that there is a time when virtually anyone can arrange to come to your salon during regularly scheduled hours. Remember that you simply cannot accommodate yourself to every single client all of the time. It is just not possible.

If you do choose to offer early drop-off or late pickup of dogs at your shop, try to coordinate these so that all the early dogs come in on one day and all the dogs who must be picked up after regular closing hours come in on another day. If you have help at the shop it might be possible to work out a schedule that allows this service to be offered on a case-by-case basis. Remember that this is a special service, not a regular one. Try not to let your customers get in the habit of making these special arrangements on a regular basis. If you do, you may as well plan to live in your grooming shop because you are certainly going to spend most of your time there.

Every client will naturally consider his to be a special case. And perhaps it is, but very few people work seven days a week for twelve or fourteen hours each day. Surely there is some time during which this client can arrange to bring his dog to the shop when the shop is normally open for business. It may take some detective work to find out just when that time is. Once you have made the determination, you should certainly note the information on the dog's record card so that you will be sure to schedule standing appointments at a time when the customer is able to bring the dog in. This is also a good reference for those customers who do not have a standing appointment. When they call to set up an appointment, you will be able to see with a glance at the card what time would be good for this particular client.

To find out what might be a good time, don't let the customer overwhelm you with his declarations that he just has to bring the dog in at 6 A.M., or that he can't possibly pick his pet up until 8 P.M. Don't hesitate to ask what sort of schedule the client has at his place of work. Be nice, be tactful, but ask. Ask what day or days the client is off work. Ask if there is a day when he goes to work a little later or, if he is going to work so early, perhaps he might be able to bring the dog in after he gets off in the afternoon (especially if you are open late one night). How about bringing the dog in during his lunch hour if he doesn't work too far from his home and your salon. It will be your job to help the client find the time when he will be able to bring the dog to your shop during hours you are open.

Naturally, there will be some times when a client simply must have his dog groomed on a specific day and absolutely cannot arrange to drop the dog off unless it can be very early, or when he just has to be able to wait until after hours to pick the dog up. This is the time when this special service comes into play. It is very important that you establish the fact that this is a special (maybe once-in-a-lifetime) service and that it is a privilege that should not be abused. Whether you make your point by stressing that this is a super favor granted only to those special few, or by charging a stiff fee for the very specialness of the service, do get the point across to the customer.

EVENING OR WEEKEND WORK

Evening or weekend work falls into the same basic category as the early drop-off or late pickup service. If you have planned your working schedule to make use of some weekend hours and some evening hours, there is very little reason for your clients to expect you to work at other evening or weekend times. If for some reason you have set up your schedule of regular hours to include only the usual 8:00 A.M. to 5:00 P.M., Monday through Friday hours, then perhaps you will wish to offer some evening or weekend work as a special service.

If you prefer to work only Monday through Friday as a general rule, then weekend grooming certainly does fall into the special services category. This is true of evening work also if you are not open late any day of the week.

Like most other things in the business of running your own grooming shop, the hours you set are your own choice. It is, of course, necessary that you keep in mind that what you are selling in your shop is service, and you must be aware that if every one of your clients had the exact same working hours that you have, some of your customers would never be able to bring their dogs in for your services.

When you elect to groom evenings and/or weekends as a special service, you should make note of that fact in your advertising and on the schedule of hours you post on your door. A line in your advertising could read simply, "Grooming evenings and weekends by special arrangement only." This should make the situation fairly clear to the customer. The very fact that this is by "special arrangement" implies that it is not a regular service and that the customer can expect to pay an extra fee for it.

When evening or weekend work is done only as a special service, it is possible to limit the number of dogs you will do during those times. If you do not choose to groom during a particular time, simply do not accept an appointment for that time.

During the times you are doing work by arrangement, you may find that if you leave your shop door unlocked you are likely to have any number of walk-in clients or just people who want to drop in to make an appointment or to ask a question. If you have no one beside yourself to answer the door, it is better to keep the door locked and the "Closed" sign prominently displayed. Don't be tempted to answer the door or you may end up being at work half the night.

In setting your fees for grooming done at special times, remember that you must set them high enough to make the extra hours worth your time. Unlike your regular work hours, you will be dealing with only one dog. This means that you will not be able to start work on a second or third dog while waiting for the first to dry. The fee you charge as an additional amount for this special time should be high enough to actually make it worth your time to stay late or to come in on one of your days off.

In order to arrive at a reasonable additional charge, compute your average hourly earnings during a normal work day, figure how long it is going to take to complete the grooming on this one dog, and add to the regular fee enough to bring your hourly wage at least up to the amount you would earn during normal hours. If you do not bring your wage up to your normal average, then you are probably working for a sum that hardly makes it advantageous for you to spend extra time at work.

OTHER EXTRAS

You may think of other special services you could offer in your area that have not been covered here. Whatever service you think of, there is sure to be someone who would like to avail himself of it. If you don't really want to provide a particular service or if it is not economically practical to offer a service, whether because of out-of-pocket expenses or because it uses up an inordinate amount of time, then don't offer the service at all.

Extra services should be just what the name implies—extra. They should be special and limited. Once a service is in general use it is no longer extra nor is it special, it is only expected. Don't hesitate to make an extra charge for those extra services. It is your time the client is asking for and you certainly deserve to be compensated for your work. With any of the special services, you may find that the client is far less interested in the service when he finds he will have to pay extra for it.

13

How Much Is It? . . .
Pricing

ONE OF YOUR concerns in your business will be pricing your services. Naturally, you will want to earn a fair wage for your time, but you will also want to make your prices both fair and consistent. It can hurt your business greatly if you charge one person one fee and another person with a similar size and type dog a different price for the same service. It is astounding how often your customers will compare notes and you can bet that they will ask questions if one finds out that another is getting your services at what appears to be a reduced rate.

One way to keep your prices consistent is to make up a price sheet. This is especially necessary if you have someone else working for you or if there are two or more of you in a partnership arrangement. It is nice to have your rates neatly typed up and placed in document protectors in a folder or notebook. In this way, if there is a question about the prices you are charging, you are able to show the customer your rates and he can see it in black and white. You will be surprised at how much authority is conveyed by the written word, even though you wrote it yourself. The very fact that you have been professional enough to take the time to make such a rate sheet will give great weight to your statements.

Another way to keep the customer informed about your rates is to make a sign or chart showing your general rates. This should be large enough to be easily read and should be prominently displayed. There are many ways to make this kind of display. You could use a sheet of poster board and felt-tip markers or tempura paint. A set of stencils will keep your lettering neat. If you are more creative, you might want to consider an attractive sign you can decorate with decoupage pictures or other permanent decorations. If you choose to make a sign board of the more permanent type, you may elect to leave the prices blank and use press-on lettering rather than a more permanent form of lettering. In this way, you can change your prices if the need should arise (and it will arise sooner or later) and you won't have to redo the entire sign. Yet another way to display your prices is to use one of the commercially available sign boards that have slots and small plastic letters and numbers. This has the advantage of being quick, easy and readily changeable.

Regardless of how you choose to keep your rates, whether in a notebook, on a sign or on a hand-lettered poster, you are going to have to make some determination of what those rates will be. As the business owner, it will be your responsibility to set the rates, and when later increases in price are indicated, you will be the one to arrive at that decision also.

In determining your rates, you will have to take a number of things into consideration. You will have to know what your overhead is going to be in terms of rent or mortgage payment, utilities, expendable supplies (such as shampoo, dip, alcohol and cleaning products) and of course, your own time. You are in this business to make a profit, not just for the fun of it. Don't fall into the trap of figuring all of your expenses and neglecting your own wages. Let's face it, if you can make substantially more money working for someone else, then why are you in business for yourself? While money is probably not the entire reason you have chosen to have a business of your own, it is certainly a factor.

Not only will you have to figure in your expenses and your own worth when planning your prices, but you will have to have a clear grasp of the amount of time it will take to perform a particular service for each breed you will be grooming in your shop. It certainly doesn't take as long to blow dry a Toy Poodle as it does to blow dry a Collie. Each factor should be taken into account when preparing your rate sheet.

INCLUSIVE PRICE

How are you going to set your prices? There are several ways and the most popular method with your clients will be an inclusive price. In most shops, an inclusive price will be the price for a complete grooming, which will include clipping, shampoo, blow dry, ear cleaning (and removing hair if necessary), toenail trimming, emptying the anal glands and any hand finishing work that might be required by that particular breed. Most shops do not include combing out mats in their inclusive price. Even though all the other things are included at a flat rate based on the size and breed of dog being groomed, most shops will add an extra charge of some sort for dogs who are in an extremely matted condition. This charge may be an hourly charge or a set amount. In some shops there is an extra charge even if the owner wants the mats cut off rather than combed out because it is more difficult to clip a matted coat. A sign should be prominently displayed in the waiting area to let customers know that there will be an extra charge for matted dogs.

Most shops also charge an additional fee for any sort of medicated shampoo or flea-and-tick dip. Again, it is important to let the customer know by means of a sign in the waiting area that these items are not part of the inclusive price schedule. It is also wise to notify the clients in the same manner that dogs who are discovered to have some kind of external parasite will be given a dip and that it will be charged in addition to the regular grooming fee.

The inclusive price is most popular with your clients because it allows them to know in advance how much this is going to cost, and they don't have to make any special decisions as to what services they want. You will find that an inclusive price saves a lot of your time in figuring the charges for each dog that is groomed in your salon and it will also save disagreements with the clients when the final bill is presented.

When pricing is inclusive, be sure to explain that a dip or mat combing will be extra. This is important even though you have signs prominently displayed on your walls. People often pay little or no attention to signs of this nature and then are surprised and displeased that the charge is higher than they had thought it was going to be. When estimating the charges for mat combing, it is always wise to overestimate. In this way the client gets a pleasant surprise when the bill is less than the original estimate.

Naturally, you will be careful to explain these things to callers who wish to have a price quoted by telephone. This is especially true if there is a question of mats and tangles. When discussing price by telephone, it is wise to refrain from quoting an exact price.

Remember that your client probably doesn't really know whether his dog is matted or not. What appears to the layman to be "a little tangled" may turn out to be a severely matted dog. When quoting by telephone, you will also want to be rather specific with regard to size limitations. The general public is not well versed in judging size as it pertains to their dog. As a rule, the owners of the larger breeds tend to believe that their dogs are larger than they really are, while the owners of the toy breeds tend to be just the opposite and often vastly underestimate the size of their pet. One common misconception is that a Poodle is a Toy because that is what the buyer was told it was going to be. In fact, many of the so called "Toy" Poodles are well into the Miniature-size category. It is a good idea to have some sort of measuring device in the reception area so that you will be able to quickly measure any dog that is questionable. In fact, one very equitable way to charge for Poodles and Poodle-type dogs is to charge a set fee per inch of the dog's height.

When planning an inclusive price list, you will do well to list alphabetically all the breeds you will be grooming. Even if some of the breeds you are trained to groom are fairly uncommon, list them anyway. It is amazing what just happens to drop in. List the price in the column next to the breed name. You may wish to do this in a rough draft and then go back and make any corrections you find necessary. You will be surprised at how the prices will work out. Some of the very large breeds will cost no more to groom than other breeds that are much smaller. At first this may look a bit out of balance, but keep in mind the difficulty of the grooming procedure required by the breed. The short-coated breeds require so little work that even though the dog might be large, he will take relatively little of your time. He will also need less drying time and thus will save your electric bill. About the only thing you might expend more of on a large short-coated dog will be water, and this is a fairly inexpensive item.

When pricing on an inclusive basis, you might wish to display a sign that states clearly exactly what is included in the base price. This sign might read: "Grooming Price Includes: Clipping, Bath, Blow Dry, Nail Trim, Ear Cleaning, Emptying Anal Glands." Below this you may wish to state "Dipping and Mat Combing Extra."

SEPARATE-ITEM PRICING

The separate-item pricing method is just what the name

suggests—each portion of the grooming is priced separately. Normally, the clipping and scissor work will be priced as one item, and bath, blow dry, toenails, anal gland emptying and ear cleaning will all be priced separately, as will special touches like nail polish or bows for a final bit of glamour. Of course, mat combing and dipping will be priced separately just as they were in the discussion of inclusive pricing.

In planning this kind of price list, it will still be necessary to make up a list that includes all of the breeds you will be grooming, but in this case you will need to list more than just a total price for each breed. You will want to list the breed and then follow with the price for clipper and scissor work, then a price for a bath and a third price for the blow dry. As a rule, ear cleaning will be the same price regardless of the breed involved, as will expressing the anal glands. The only difference here might be a slightly higher charge for those breeds that must have the hair pulled out of the ears. Toenails are usually priced by size category so that the price for nails would usually be listed by small, medium, large and giant breeds.

As you can see, computing a total price when charges are made for each separate service can get complicated. There is, of course, much more room for error when pricing with this method. When using this method of pricing it is very important that you write down exactly what the client wishes to have done so that there will be no question when the final bill is presented. The client will have to make several decisions. He will have to decide exactly which services he wishes to have done during this visit and which are not to be done.

There are some very real disadvantages in separate-item pricing. In an effort to economize, you may find that some of your clients will decide to give the dog his bath at home rather than pay you to do the bathing. While this may be a bit easier on the client's pocketbook, you may find that the dog is not thoroughly clean or brushed out properly and thus you are at a real disadvantage in trying to make the dog look nice. The client may also miss the fact that his dog has fleas or ticks and now you are in the position of having to tell the customer that the dog is still going to have to have a bath and a dip to rid him of these parasites.

One compromise between inclusive pricing and separate-item pricing is the use of a base-price list that is essentially inclusive, and then have a separate-item price list that lists certain extras such as toenail trim, nail polish and ribbons or bows. This gives the customer a chance to make some choices, but it will keep him from cutting corners on more important items, and by doing so hamper your efforts to turn out a good-quality grooming job. It will also keep the client from shortchanging his dog of some of the needed services, such as ear cleaning or anal gland emptying, that can be important to the dog's health.

PRICING SPECIAL SERVICES

Now is the time to give serious thought to the pricing of the extra services that were discussed in Chapter 12. While it would be nice to be able to include all the little extras for your clients at no additional charge, you will either have to charge a high enough price for grooming services to cover the extras or plan to be a nonprofit agency. You can also run yourself ragged trying to please everyone all of the time.

When pricing various extra services, you must be very realistic in what the service is costing you in time and in actual cash outlay. This can mean the difference between success and failure in a service business. If you want to give a special service to a client on an occasional basis, you need not count the cost. It is when the special services become a regular item that the cost must be taken into account.

Some of the special services you might offer to your customers really will not cost you anything in the way of a cash outlay. Evening and weekend grooming is a good example of this type of service. You are not having to spend any extra money for your building or for your utilities just because you are doing some portion of your work at a nonregular time. The cost that must be taken into account for this kind of service is the cost to your own well-being. People need their own private time as well as time for their work. When work becomes all-consuming, sometimes the individual finds that his entire lifestyle gets out of balance. Here is an excellent opportunity to offer a special service at no real cost to you that will give you a real opportunity to develop good customer relations. When charging for evening or weekend work, simply set the regular fee plus a certain amount for the "special service." Then be sure that your hours are such that you still have the time that you need for your own personal activities.

The fee that you choose to set for an early arrival or a late pickup will have to depend entirely on the value you place on your own time. Like evening or weekend grooming, coming in early or staying late will hardly cost you anything in actual cash so long as you are providing the service yourself; the cost is in your own time. If you would like to offer this service and you feel that it is one that will be enough in demand, you might elect to hire someone part-time to come in early or to be at your salon later than the normal closing hour on specific days each week. By doing this, you can arrange all of the early or late clients for those days when you have extra help. To figure the cost for this service, simply figure the wage you will be paying for your part-time help and base your charge to the client on that figure. By all means, do not hesitate to give yourself a healthy profit on this service. Don't forget that it is a real convenience to the client and that your planning and preparation allow you to offer the service to the customer.

The cost of offering a feeding while the dog is at your salon is a bit more involved than some of the other special items. If you choose to offer this service, you will have to figure in the cost of the food itself, the dishes, your time to prepare and serve the food, the cost and the time involved in dishwashing and of course the extra time involved in making sure that the well-fed dogs do not soil themselves. It is easiest to figure the actual cash outlay and hardest to figure the cost of your time and inconvenience. The cost per dog in cash outlay is not going to be a staggering figure, but the inconvenience may be. Whether this service should be offered at all will be your own choice as will your decision as to the charge you should make for it. You may rest assured that while your clientele may think this a delightful service, they will not be pleased to pay a large sum for it. One way to compromise on this service is to offer a snack-type treat to each dog. Always ask the permission of the client to give his dog a treat because you should have his approval, and asking lets the client know that his dog will be receiving this treat. You can easily afford to stock several types of treats and because these small snacks are inexpensive there would be no need to charge the client at all. The other advantage to using a treat instead of a full meal is that the dogs will not be so full that they will need to relieve themselves. Another way to accomplish this is to give the treat to the owner to give to the dog when it is picked up. The client will be just as impressed as if the dog had been fed a meal, and your reputation will get a maximum boost with a minimum outlay in time, effort or cash.

Pickup and delivery service is the one service that is likely to be most in demand with your clientele. Because this is such a convenience, the client will usually be more than willing to pay for it. Although pickup and delivery is the most popular service you can offer as an extra, it is also the one service that is going to be the most expensive to you both in cash outlay and in time. If you choose to do all the pickup and delivery yourself (or if you are in the position of having to do it), you absolutely must figure your own hourly wage into the cost of providing this service or you will be losing money. The time you spend driving around picking up or delivering dogs could be spent in your shop grooming dogs or taking calls for appointments.

In figuring the cost of this service, you will need to prorate the cost of vehicle use, insurance coverage, fuel and maintenance costs and the wage of the driver (whether it is your own time or the time of an employee you are paying). It would be to your advantage to consider the distances involved in arranging your charges. One way to figure distances into your fees is to use a map of the area in which you will be providing the service. On the map, locate your salon and then draw a series of concentric circles around your own location. Set the circles a specific distance apart (whether in blocks or in miles) and let each circle be a price zone. In this way, you can be sure that every client will be charged an equitable fee for the distance involved as well as the time it takes to make the drive. Do not forget when figuring the cost of this service that you will be making each trip twice—once to get the dog and once to take it home again.

In actual practice, it will be a little less expensive to offer this service if you are picking up several dogs at one time, even though they may be in different areas. You will be able to plan your routes so that a minimum of time and fuel are expended. In planning the charges for this service however, it is necessary for you to plan the charge to each zone as if you were only going to pick up one dog on each trip. This is true because there will almost certainly be times when that is exactly what is going to happen. In that case, you would be losing money if you had neglected to figure your costs on a one-dog-per-trip basis. If you are picking up more than one dog you will be making money and that is why you are in business.

DETERMINING THE USUAL RATE

When planning your price schedule for grooming and for the other services you may be offering in your shop, you will find it a real help to have some general idea about what is being charged by other grooming shops in your area. It is to be hoped that you are on good terms with the other groomers in your area. This will certainly make it easier to find out what they are charging for their work. Remember too that grooming is often available at veterinary clinics and at boarding kennels. These places should be considered when you are thinking of determining what the prevailing prices are.

One way to find out prices at the various shops in your vicinity is to call around and ask about prices as if you have a dog you wished to have groomed. This is a sketchy technique at best, but it will at least give you some sort of idea about the general range of prices. While this is not a terriby complete or accurate method of determining prices, it can suffice if you are unwilling to make a better effort.

Probably the very best policy that you can pursue in learning what the other shops in your area are charging for their various services is to simply be honest with the owners or managers of these shops and *ask*. You may find that some of the people to whom you speak will be a bit taken aback that you are approaching them about this subject, but most of them will answer your questions if you are tactful in the asking. One nice way to make this approach is to say to the owner or manager, "I am planning on opening a new shop and I certainly don't want to cause hard feelings by undercharging for our services." This lets your competitors know that you are interested in making a fair profit and that you are more than willing to compete on a reasonable basis rather than by undercutting prices in order to draw the clientele away from other places of business. There seems to be quite a lot of jealousy among dog groomers and it is a shame that this is the case. Like any independent business, competition is the very life blood of the dog-grooming business. After all, no one shop is going to be able to please every single customer and the very customer another groomer simply hates to see come through the door could turn out to be one of your very favorites. All too few groomers seem to recognize this as a real fact of the business world.

Often, veterinarians will offer some sort of grooming service simply because it is in demand and they don't have a shop to which they would like to send their patients. If you get acquainted with some of the veterinarians in your area, you may find that they will be more than happy to tell you what their prices are and in some cases will be delighted to have someone to whom they can refer people who want more extensive grooming for their dogs than the clinic is able to provide.

Boarding kennels, like veterinary hospitals, may only provide a minimal grooming service for their clientele because the clients demand it. It is possible that you might be able to work closely with one or more of the kennels in your area in such a way that it would benefit both you and the kennel. Mutual referrals can be the basis for a sound business relationship. If the kennel in question has only limited grooming services available, you might be able to profit greatly from being on their list as a shop they might recommend to their clients.

PRICE RANGE

There are several ways to look at pricing. One of course is the low-price, high-volume method of pricing. When using this budget method of pricing, you must plan to be able to render a reasonable service at a lower cost than is available at most of the places in your general area. This method of pricing means that you will have to be ready to turn out more work on any given day in order to make a reasonable profit. There are shops that operate quite successfully on this basis. Often these are "no frills" establishments. While they may be clean and well maintained, there may be very little in the way of decoration or embellishment. These shops often dispense with the little extras like ribbon, bows, nail polish or cologne. They specialize in very plain style clips also and usually do a minimal amount of scissor-finishing work. As a rule, the dogs turned out by these shops are clean, neatly clipped, and free of parasites, but they do not generally sport any of the fancier clips that might be done at other shops. The customer who frequents this sort of shop is usually more budget conscious than the patrons at some of the more posh salons, but is concerned that his dog is well cared for and that it is kept in good condition. The extras are not especially important to this client, but he does want good basic care. This client does appreciate concern and he wants to feel that his dog is treated well even if the work done is more practical than deluxe. A few people will shy away from this kind of shop simply because it seems too cheap.

Most shops will fall into a sort of middle-of-the-road category. In this type of pricing, your prices will usually fall into a pattern similar to the bulk of the other shops within your geographical region. The prices may be slightly higher on some things and slightly lower on others, but will average out to just about the same as most of the other area groomers. The middle-of-the-road shop doesn't have to rely entirely on volume to produce a reasonable profit margin, but can expect to render a little more individualized care than the budget shop. In this shop there will certainly be some extras, but the groomer will not plan to spend an inordinate amount of time on each dog.

The clientele at the middle-of-the-road shop will also be a fairly average group. Some will be more budget-minded than others, some will expect a few more frills, but all are likely to want good care and concern for their pets. This is a shop where the clients are usually from a wide range of economic levels, but most take good care of their dogs and try to see that they are kept in reasonably good condition between groomings.

Undoubtedly, this midrange pricing is the most common method of pricing practiced. This is a good sound basis for a business that will grow and prosper, building over the years. Customers feel they are not being overcharged and are receiving good service, and they tend to be loyal to the shop and recommend it to others.

The last price range is the elite or "snob appeal" price range. From a business standpoint this is the most risky method, but when it works it can be very lucrative. The elite shop specializes in service with a capital "S." For a price, this shop will usually provide the client's dog with any number of little extras, most of which mean little or nothing to the dog, but which make the owner happy.

When using this method of pricing, as a rule the price for any given item will be at the very top of the scale for any shop in the area and will be higher on most items. The whole success that is enjoyed by this kind of shop is based on the "if it is that expensive it has to be good" line of thinking. This kind of shop will thrive best in a large metropolitan area where there is an abundance of affluent clients to draw from.

The elite shop usually will groom relatively few dogs on any given day but will spend extra time with each dog and spare nothing when it comes to the little extras. These shops may be downright ostentatious in their decor and will often tend toward being a bit syrupy in attitude, but for some clients, this is exactly the right atmosphere. The client who patronizes this sort of shop wants to feel elite. He doesn't mind paying for the services, but they had better be good. The client at the elite shop may be faithful to a particular shop for many years, but one insult or one time when he feels less than special and he may drop the shop like a hot potato. The clients at this kind of shop must be catered to in many ways. On the other hand, the clients here do expect that the shop will have some rules that will be strictly enforced simply because it is an elite establishment. The standing appointment rule is one that is often enforced by this kind of salon. Many of these shops will absolutely insist that every dog have a standing appointment and that those appointments must be kept.

It may take a bit longer to establish this kind of salon, but if you enjoy this kind of situation, the elite shop may be exactly what you want. This is a situation in which good contacts can be of great value. It only takes a few of the right kinds of recommendations from the right people to put a shop on the map and well on its way to being a real gold mine.

No matter which of the price ranges you choose to use in your place of business, be sure that it is one with which you are personally satisfied. If you are not happy with your pricing, you are going to feel uncomfortable when you quote prices to the customer and the customer in turn will feel uneasy. This never helps a business. Be sure that you are doing what is right for you and for your business and you can expect your clientele will feel that it is right for them.

14

Business Is Terrific . . .

Expanding Your Operation

WHEN THE DAY comes that you find you have so much business that there is no way you can keep up with the demand for your services, it is time to start thinking about expanding your operation. This is a wonderful predicament to be in and one most business owners hope will occur early in their business careers.

Expansion can be a mixed blessing. This is especially true if you have had little experience in a supervisory position. The very fact that your business has grown to the point where expansion is becoming necessary is proof that you have certainly been doing some things right and it would be a real shame to lose that special something by expanding too much, too quickly. This is a problem that sometimes occurs in a young and successful business, and when the business later goes downhill, no one seems to know why. It is better to expand bit by bit and let the business build as you grow. In this way, you can avoid some of the stress of rapid expansion and maintain your personal touch in your business.

LET SOMEONE ELSE DO THE WASHING

The first step in expanding your grooming business might be to hire someone to do bathing, brushing and drying. This is fairly simple work and you should be able to find someone who can learn it within a short period of time. It is important that you be sure to let the person you hire know exactly how you want the work done and to be quite firm (but reasonable) in your demands.

In selecting someone to work as a bath/brush person in your salon you will have some important choices to make. You may be able to find someone who has done this kind of work before in another salon. That is all well and good. The question is, does the person do things the way you want them done? This is important. If you cannot take charge of the situation right from the very beginning, then the situation will soon take charge of you and you will not be comfortable. This is not to imply that an experienced individual is not desirable. In fact, an experienced person may have good ideas to offer and it certainly pays to keep an open mind. It is necessary however, that an employee/employer relationship be established and maintained. How strict this relationship is will be an individual matter. For some people, it is easier to maintain this relationship at a fairly formal level so that they can feel comfortable in giving orders to the employee. For others a more relaxed atmosphere is just as comfortable.

Perhaps you will prefer to begin with an inexperienced person and train that person to do things the way you prefer to have them done. With an inexperienced person, there are no bad habits to be broken. This can be a real advantage to you. It can be very irritating and disruptive to continually have to correct work. In fairness to the employee, you must understand that it can be difficult to learn a new way of doing things. Training a person to do the baths and blow dry the dogs you will be grooming requires that you be prepared to be a teacher. You will have to be ready to analyze, step by step, exactly what it is you do and how you want it done.

The inexperienced person will require the most basic kind of instruction, from how to hold a dog, to how to get it into the bath tub, to how to apply the shampoo. There are far more details than meet the eye. This can be a confusing time for the new employee as well as a frustrating time for you. Be prepared at first to have your new employee working at a much slower rate than you are accustomed to working yourself. This is natural. When you first started, it took you a longer time to complete each task than it does now. Sometimes it is easy to forget how much there is to learn in the dog-grooming business and how long it took you to learn it.

One useful aid to teaching a brand-new person how to do your bath and brush work is a small chart or card that can be posted above the tub with every step in bathing listed in order. This is no substitute for your own personal instruction, but it is valuable for the new employee and will save a lot of questions. A similar list could be posted in the area where prebath work and blow drying are done. Again, list each step in order so that the new employee can refer to the list to be sure that the work is being completed correctly.

Having someone who will do all the bathing and blow drying for you can increase your daily output by a substantial margin. You will be surprised at how much more you can get done when you are able to eliminate these steps from the work you must do on each dog. These steps tend to be the most time consuming part of dog grooming and at the same time are the least technical.

The way you choose to determine a salary for your new employee will depend on several factors. If you intend this person to do nothing except baths and blow drys, then you may want to consider a piece-work basis for payment. When you pay the employee a certain amount per dog done, you will find that, as a rule, speed is picked up fairly quickly. The only hazard in this method of payment is that the untrained individual may be so intent on turning out numbers of dogs in order to fatten his paycheck that he neglects to maintain adequate levels of quality in his work. You will certainly need to keep a close eye on that factor because it is your reputation that is at stake and dogs returned to the owners in less than absolutely clean condition will damage the reputation of your business.

If you expect the person you hire to do other things besides the bath/brush work, then you will probably need to plan on paying an hourly wage. In this case, you will have to be the judge as to exactly what you expect the employee to do and how many hours per day you can afford to have this help. If your shop is really growing, you may find that it will be more than worth your time to have someone full-time who will do bath/blow-dry work and who will also assume some of the cleaning chores. You are more valuable to your business for your talents as a groomer and manager than as a janitor.

When planning to hire someone to work in your shop, be sure that you examine carefully the state employment laws so that you will know what your obligations are as an employer. These may vary depending on whether you are hiring someone as a part-time employee or as a full-time employee. There also may be some variations if you are paying on a piece-work basis rather than an hourly wage. It will be important to you to know these things.

Information about these items should be available to you from your state employment commission.

Insurance is also important to you when you have someone else working for you. You will need to be sure that the insurance coverage you have will be adequate to cover employees, and that you are protected in the event one of your employees is negligent in his care of one of the dogs in your shop. You will also need to be sure that you have adequate protection should the employee somehow suffer an injury while on your premises. Your insurance agent should be able to help you with all the details necessary for a good insurance program, and he will be your best source of information with regard to your insurance needs. Just as it is important that you plan for good insurance coverage when you first think of opening a grooming salon, so it is important that you upgrade that coverage so that it is adequate to meet your expanded needs.

A RECEPTIONIST MIGHT BE IN ORDER

Some of the larger salons are busy enough to hire someone who does nothing except answer the telephone, make appointments, receive dogs from the clients as they arrive and return dogs to the owners when they are done. In order for this to be practical, your shop must be doing a big business.

In selecting someone to fill a receptionist position, it will be necessary for you to interview carefully because the position title might be misleading. Not every person who might answer an advertisement for a position of this nature will be capable of dealing with dogs. Many otherwise well-qualified applicants will fail in the role of dog handler. Even though your receptionist will not be doing the actual grooming work, it will still be necessary that he or she be someone who is comfortable with dogs and who can handle them in a calm and capable manner. This person should also be able to take direction well and be able to relay information accurately because much of the time you will have to answer questions and have the answer relayed to the caller.

When planning to hire a receptionist, you will want to choose someone who will make a nice impression on your customers. This doesn't mean that you must hire someone who is a candidate for beauty queen, but rather someone who is friendly, outgoing and neat in appearance. Like your front entrance and your waiting room, your receptionist is part of that all-important first impression that means so much to the success of your business. A sloppy or rude receptionist can cause damage that may take months to undo.

If you have chosen to wear a particular uniform in your place of business, you should certainly plan on having the receptionist wear the same uniform, or a variation of it that will be recognizable to your clients. If you are wearing a grooming jacket over a plain shirt and a pair of slacks, you might want the receptionist to wear the same color and style jacket over regular clothing. One tip: Even though the receptionist will not be grooming, he or she will still be coming into contact with dogs, and clothing and footgear should be appropriate. Women should not try to wear high-heeled shoes because it is very difficult to lead or control a large or boisterous dog and walk in high heels at the same time.

When hiring either a bath/brush person or a receptionist, you may want to consider hiring more than one person to fill each position. If you are in an area where there is a college or university, it is often possible to hire students at a reasonable wage, but full-time work for them can present scheduling problems. Don't rule out the possibility of hiring one person to work in the morning and another to work afternoons or hiring people to work on alternate days. If your shop is open late on one or more evenings each week, or if you are open weekends, even more possibilities occur along these lines. There are many people available who might wish to work part-time only. In this way, you can find the people you need to cover the amount of time you need to cover. Be flexible in your thinking and you will find that you will be better able to take advantage of the various opportunities that present themselves to you.

HIRING ANOTHER GROOMER

If you are in a good location and you manage your business well, the time will come when you are not going to be able to handle all the business coming your way, even with someone doing all the bathing and blow drying, and someone else acting as receptionist. When that time comes, you will have to decide whether or not you want to keep your shop small or expand by bringing in another groomer to work for you. If you want to keep your shop small and do all the grooming yourself, then you have reached the happy situation where you are able to set up a list of standing appointments and can be very insistent that those appointments be kept. Ideally, you will have a waiting list of would-be clients who want to be called if one of your much-sought-after standing-appointment times becomes available. If this is your goal, then you have arrived and congratulations are in order.

If, on the other hand, you would like to expand your business and hire someone else to work in your salon, you are now faced with a whole new set of choices. The same decision you had to make when looking for someone to do bath/brush work will now apply again. Do you wish to hire someone who is already a trained or experienced dog groomer or do you want someone you can train yourself?

Hiring a Trained Groomer

Because this position is so much more responsible than the position of bath/brush person, you will have to screen potential employees very carefully. It may come as quite a surprise to you to find just how little some people who claim to be experienced know about dog grooming. Because most states do not require any sort of license to groom dogs and because there is no educational requirement as such, virtually anyone who cares to do so can represent himself as a dog groomer.

When seeking someone to work for you who is already trained as a groomer you will want to ask some very searching questions. It will be important to you to find out just where the prospective employee was trained and by whom. Has this person had any actual experience or did all of his training come from a book or by correspondence? Has he worked for anyone else in your immediate area? Does he have any references? It will be necessary for you to know the limits of the applicant's abilities and knowledge. Your salon reputation can stand or fall on the capabilities of the groomer you hire. Don't be in a rush and don't consider it out of line to ask numerous questions. The time to be careful and take your time is before you hire someone. It is much easier not to hire an individual at all than it is to have to fire that person later.

When conducting your interviews of prospective groomers, don't hesitate to ask that the person give you an actual demonstration of his grooming abilities. If it is going to take this individual four hours to do one small dog then you will not profit yourself much in hiring him. You will want to keep a careful eye on the interviewee if you allow him to do his demonstration work on one of your client's dogs. It would be better if you could ask the person to bring along a dog or if you could call a friend, explain what you are doing and offer to groom the dog for them at no charge so that the person you are interviewing will have a dog to use for his demonstration.

Don't get in a hurry when looking for a groomer to hire. Remember that this is your own business that you have worked hard to develop. You want someone who will be a credit to your reputation. It is far better to take your time, find someone who has the talent and the reliability you need and then hire that person rather than just take the first person to answer your ad.

One way to ease the initial steps in locating a new groomer is to list the opening with an employment agency. When you list with an agency, you can specify from the beginning exactly what qualifications you consider basic to the position. In this way, you let the agency do much of the preliminary screening for you. You will save hours on the telephone and hours more interviewing totally unsuitable applicants.

One way to simplify your interview is to make up an application form of your own and have some copies made for use when you have a prospective groomer to interview. This will allow you to get all the general information about the applicant together with any specific information you have decided is necessary to help you choose exactly the right individual. Because the grooming business is unique, you will find that your questionnaire may be a little different from the job application forms you have seen before. A written application also has the advantage of demonstrating the applicant's handwriting and shows whether or not he is able to follow directions.

After you have had the applicant fill out the application, have held a personal interview and have seen a demonstration of the applicant's work, you will want to let the individual know that you will call and let him know your decision. This gives you time to review the application in depth, to think about the applicant and to give serious thought to the entire impression you have formed about this person. It will also give you time to interview other applicants. Do not feel obligated to give the applicant an answer right on the spot. Other businesses don't, so why should you? The exception to this might be the applicant who is totally unsuitable for your needs. If this is the case, and it is immediately obvious, it would be good manners to simply state that you feel this position would not be right for him and that you don't want to keep him in suspense. In this way, the individual is free to look elsewhere and you are spared the necessity to call him back to give him the news.

You will find that there will be some differences in grooming style between groomers. This is normal and should not cause a problem. If you feel that a particular style just doesn't fit in with the work you expect to turn out in your establishment, you will have to decide whether this applicant is basically a well-trained groomer who could adjust to your needs, or if he is simply not right for your place of business. It is unlikely that you will find anyone who grooms exactly the way you do. It is important that you recognize this fact when looking for a groomer to hire. If you expect to find someone whose work is a carbon copy of your own, then your search for a new groomer is doomed to failure.

In considering the various applicants who will come to you, keep in mind the impression you wish to make on the public and ask yourself if this person conveys that impression. Be sure to look carefully at the handwriting on the application form. If the applicant cannot write legibly and spell reasonably well, your card file is sure to suffer. What a waste of time to have to ask to have entries on the cards deciphered. Naturally, you will expect any of your employees to be able to hold a reasonable conversation, to have good telephone manners, and to be polite to your customers as well as handle dogs and give good service.

If you find someone you think suitable, one way to give yourself the opportunity to know this individual a little better and to be able to make a more thorough observation of his work is to hire him on a trial basis for a specified period of time. If you hire a groomer for two weeks or one month on a trial basis, you will be able to see a wide variety of work done and you will be better able to determine whether you will want to work with this person on a permanent basis.

When you have decided on a groomer to hire, call that person and notify him of your decision. (This is also the time to call all the other applicants who were under consideration and let them know that you have hired someone for a trial period. Ask at that time whether or not they wish to be kept in your file for future reference. If the first individual you try doesn't work out, you will have several others to try.) Be sure to have your new groomer come in for a morning or an afternoon orientation period. At that time, discuss salary or commission and any benefits you may plan to offer. Let there be no question in the person's mind as to what day is payday, what equipment you will furnish and what equipment you expect the groomer to supply. Let him know what uniform is to be worn and who will provide it. If you will be paying on a percentage basis, let your new employee know exactly what percentage to expect. Be sure to explain any deductions that will be taken out of the paycheck. This is also the time to be very specific about the days and hours you expect the groomer to work.

In general, let the new groomer know exactly what to expect from this job. If you are hiring this individual on a trial basis, be very explicit about that fact. Any new job is stressful. By being as specific as possible and by letting the new employee know exactly what is expected, you will help to relieve that stress and get this new relationship off to a good start.

Training a New Groomer

It is inevitable that no matter who you hire to work in your shop, at least some training will be required, but it is also possible that you will be unable to find anyone who is trained to groom or who can meet your standards. In this event, you will be faced with the need to train someone from the ground up.

Finding a prospect to train as a groomer can be even more difficult than finding the right groomer among several experienced applicants. When looking for someone to train, you will be gambling on the individual's capability to learn and develop as the sort of groomer you will wish to have working in your shop. You will also be gambling on your ability to teach that person adequately.

When you begin looking for a trainee, you are likely to be overwhelmed with applicants whose sole qualification is that they "just *love* dogs." Unfortunately, this is probably one of the least necessary traits to seek in a qualified applicant. Naturally, you will look for many of the same general characteristics in a trainee that you would expect to find in a trained groomer. If the applicant is not clean and good mannered at the outset, he is not likely to develop these traits at a later date. You will expect someone who is able to write legibly and who can read and follow directions. The trainee should be a hard worker who is eager to learn and who is not afraid of dirty work or lifting a heavy dog.

Once you have established that the applicant has met the basic educational requirements and that he seems to be a likely candidate for training, you will simply have to gamble on many of the other factors involved. About the only practical test you might be able to give to an individual who hopes to learn grooming is to watch the person with dogs of different sizes and types. Ask the applicant to take a dog out of a crate and to place it on the table, for instance. You can observe the general way in which he approaches and touches the dog. In making this request you will of course choose a dog that is relatively easy to handle and not likely to bite, in order to avoid the possibility of an injury to the applicant. If possible, find out whether this person is uncomfortable with any particular breed or breeds. While this would not necessarily rule out an otherwise likely prospect, it will at least give you a bit more insight into the sort of person with whom you are dealing. If possible, you might wish to confront a fearful individual with a gentle dog of the breed that makes him uncomfortable and see whether it is possible for him to work with the dog even though he might be somewhat apprehensive. If the applicant refuses to even try to approach or handle certain breeds, you may want to reconsider his suitability.

In planning to hire a trainee groomer, the matter of salary will inevitably arise. Remember that you will be providing this person with a trade that can lead to a good income. Remember also that college students are not paid to attend college nor do students at a beauty college receive wages for their studies. Naturally, most of the people who apply to you as trainee prospects will be doing so because they need to have a job. This poses a rather thorny problem. You will be taking up your time to teach the trainee, yet he needs to earn a wage. One way to resolve this problem is to teach the trainee how to bathe and blow dry dogs and then pay him a set fee per dog while he is in the process of learning the balance of the grooming procedure. While this won't allow the trainee a large salary it will at least help out.

If possible, you may want to consider taking on a trainee well in advance of the time when it appears you will be in serious need of another groomer to work in your shop. As you well know, dog grooming is not learned in a short period of time. Depending on the number of breeds customarily groomed in your salon, it could take up to a year to have a new groomer properly trained so that he would be a credit to your establishment.

To make things easier on the trainee financially, it might be possible to complete his training on one specific breed and then arrange a salary based on commissions for dogs of the breed he grooms. Another way to accomplish the same general end is to pay a set wage for a certain number of hours of general work, such as janitorial work, each week and do the training as well. If you are well enough known and your expertise is such that you are well respected in your field, you can also take on apprentices to train with the understanding that their pay is their education. These trainees would be in essentially the same position as students at a beauty college. They would be expected to render services to the various dogs as they learned to perform those services, and they would do so under your supervision. This is a time-consuming way to train a new groomer, but it can be an extremely satisfactory way to develop a groomer who will work to your exact specifications, and who will turn out work that will be a credit to your business. At first an apprentice will tend to be very slow and you may wonder why you ever tried this kind of project. Have patience. It can be most satisfying to see a trainee grow in ability and knowledge.

If you choose to train a groomer for your shop, it will be necessary for you to sit down and plan a basic training program based on the breeds groomed in your shop. You will need to begin with the most basic information imaginable and progress slowly and carefully through the various steps in grooming. Remember your own learning process. Possibly there are things you have learned since your initial involvement in grooming that will make it easier for you to teach a trainee this work. There is nothing too basic for this type of program. If you are not sure about how to teach a particular step, write down the instructions and then follow those instructions yourself. Follow them to the letter and see if the result is what you want it to be. If not, then the instructions are not complete. It is so easy to forget how little the beginner knows and you must gear your instructions to the person who knows nothing whatsoever about dog grooming.

Don't be discouraged away from training a groomer for your salon. This can be one of the most challenging efforts you will undertake, and if done well, it will be one of your most satisfying efforts. You can take great pride in being able to say that all of the groomers in your salon are people you have trained yourself so that your clients can have good consistent service. This is a real plus for your business.

You will learn a good deal from your first experience in teaching grooming. Teaching will force you to analyze the work you do. At first you may be astounded as your pupil blithely skips steps in the work. If something is left undone, it is very probably an error in your teaching. Perhaps you didn't place enough emphasis on the step omitted by the student. Fortunately, teaching will become easier as you go along. Not only will your groomer trainee be gaining in knowledge and ability, but you will be developing your skills in teaching. The first trainee is certainly going to be the most difficult for you. Subsequent trainees will generally be easier for you to teach because you are already an experienced teacher. You will also learn to recognize an individual who has potential when you are interviewing prospects.

In teaching grooming, do not be afraid to be demanding. It is your salon, your business and your reputation that will suffer if sloppy work is turned out. Your clients have come to expect a certain level of expertise from you and they will expect to get the same quality no matter who does the work.

Your Clients Want You

One situation that will occur whether you hire an experienced groomer or train someone from the ground up, is that clients all expect *you* to groom their dogs. Remember that every client feels he is special. In fact, you have gone out of your way to make your clients feel they are very important to you. Each client is going to expect that you will do his dog even if you don't do any other grooming at all. Some of your customers will be quite insistent on this point. The only thing you are going to be able to do about this is simply recommend your new groomer with great conviction and convince the client that this person will do just as nice a job as you would, and that you will be checking to make sure that the work is done as you have always done it.

When you have a new groomer, it is extremely important that you be able to give that groomer a sincere recommendation. If you are not able to really give honest praise to the ability of the groomer, then perhaps you should consider looking further for a groomer to work in your salon. Even though a trained groomer will do some things a bit differently, you absolutely must be convinced that this is a groomer worthy of your place of business and one who will turn out work that will meet your standards and satisfy your clients.

Yet Another Groomer

As your business continues to build and to grow, you may find that yet another groomer is needed. What a terrific situation. If your business is doing this well, you can be pleased and proud of the job you are doing. By now, you will find that you spend more time on administrative tasks than you have before, but it is to be hoped that the actual functioning of your salon is going along smoothly.

Whether you choose to hire or train your next groomer, you will find the job easier because of the experience you have had before. In fact, with each subsequent new employee that you hire, whether it is a groomer, a bath/brush person, a receptionist or simply someone to perform janitorial work, you will find that you are developing your skills at choosing people who will work out well for you in your particular shop.

OPENING ANOTHER SHOP

The day will come when your salon will no longer be large enough to accommodate even one more groomer. You will have reached the physical limits of space for more workers or more dogs. This is the time to decide whether to stop where you are, to seek larger quarters or to go on to the next step—opening another shop.

If you decide to open another grooming salon, you will have the exciting opportunity to go back to somewhat the same situation you were in when you made your initial decision to open a business of your own, except that now you are armed with all the knowledge you have gained through your experience in opening a shop and running it. You will have learned a great deal from the work you have done so far and will be much better prepared to look for a new location, plan decor and do all the other tasks that go into launching a new grooming salon.

Somebody Has To Be the Manager

The primary difference in opening a second shop (and eventually a third or fourth) is that you will have to step out of your situation as a groomer and assume the role of general manager. You will no longer be able to devote most of your personal working time to the grooming itself, but will instead be in a supervisory capacity and will act as a quality controller for the work done in your salons.

216

Now that you are delegating most of the actual grooming work, it is also going to be necessary for you to delegate some of the actual authority as well. As long as you are involved in only one salon, it is thoroughly practical for you to do all the managing, make all the decisions and be on top of the situation. Once you are the owner of two or more shops, it is critical that you have in each of your shops a well-trained and responsible individual to work as manager. This is not to say that the person you choose to act as manager of your shop or shops is not a dog groomer. The person who manages a shop for you should certainly be someone who is skilled at grooming and who can guide and direct any other groomers who are working at that shop, but he or she must have other skills as well.

When you select someone to be manager in one of your shops, you will be giving that person a tremendous responsibility. Everything the manager does is a direct reflection on you and on your business. The salon manager is your representative. It is very important that this be a person you trust implicitly to make decisions you have made up until this point. If you cannot trust this individual to make a good, sound decision, then do not select him to be a manager. Keep in mind that when you open a second shop, you are not going to need just one manager, you will need two. It is very difficult to act as manager in one salon and at the same time competently oversee the management of a second shop. You will need to be able to divide your time between the two locations without neglecting either of them.

It is to be hoped that by now you have several groomers working for you with whom you are pleased and who do a great job in your salon. Ideally, when you are thinking of selecting managers for your new shop and for your present location, you will be able to promote two of the people who are already working for you to the position of manager. This will give you the necessary freedom to start work on the new salon and at the same time will allow you to supervise the new managers until they are established in that position.

The time to start thinking of a manager for the second salon is the time you start thinking of opening a second salon, so you will be looking for two people with the capability to groom and accept the responsibilities of management. At the same time, you may want to start looking for some other people to train as groomers for the new shop. If all this sounds premature, remember how long it took to find someone to work for you or how long it took to train a new groomer.

Where Will the New Shop Be?

If you are in a large city, it may be possible to have several shops that do not overlap in clientele. If you live in a small town, you may have to think about expanding your operation into a neighboring town in order to avoid giving your first shop too much competition. There is no point in having two separate shops that function as one. If that is the situation, then you probably do not need to open a second salon at all, but need instead to seek a larger facility. For the sake of this discussion, however, let us assume that you are going to open a second shop rather than simply move into larger quarters with your present business.

You are in an excellent position to analyze the situation and to decide on a second location. Some of the factors that will affect your decision will be similar to factors you had to consider when planning your first shop, and some will be slightly different. Zoning and the availability of a building will affect your choice of location just as they did initially. The location itself will take the same kind of consideration that you gave to the choice of your present location with regard to area and accessibility.

When planning a second salon, you must give thought to the distribution of your clientele. If you have a substantial number of clients from a particular geographical area, especially one that is a long way from your present location, then you might wish to give serious consideration to seeking a business location in that area. Perhaps a number of your clients come from a neighboring town to have their dogs groomed at your shop. Why not look at the idea of opening a shop in that town. One way to check the distribution of the clients who are currently patronizing your establishment is to use a large map and push pins. With the map mounted on a wall, put a pin into every block where one of your clients lives. Using your card file, this should be a fairly simple task. This will allow you to see at a glance where the bulk of your clients are located. You will be able to "pinpoint" any other areas that contain large numbers of your clientele, and thus will be able to start thinking about the general direction in which you should look to find a location for your new shop. By now, you should have enough experience in running your business to be able to do good research on a prospective location.

You will, of course, be contacting the various veterinarians in the area in which you are thinking of locating your new establishment and you will certainly contact any kennels or pet-supply stores in the vicinity. You will be better able to judge now the kind of building that would best serve your needs. Your experience will be your guide with regard to the things you feel you must have in this shop, and the things you can easily dispense with.

You As the General Manager

One thing you must consider when opening a second shop is your own time. As your business has expanded, you have seen your role shift from that of shop owner/groomer to shop owner/manager. Now you are going to see a further shift in your work. You will probably be doing very little of the actual grooming work in either of your shops, and as time goes on, it is to be hoped that more and more of the business activities within each shop will be delegated to the managers of the shops instead of your doing them yourself.

If the managers are going to be handling the business aspect of the shops as well as managing the groomers, then what will you as owner be doing? You will become the General Manager, and as such, you will be concerned with managing the managers. You will certainly be spending time in each of the shops and will be handling the major business decisions. You will set the general tone and policies for your shops. It will be important for you to keep your own aims and goals at the forefront. You will want to keep in touch with the needs of your clients and to see that those needs are being met via the policies of your establishment.

If you are wise, you will help your managers to grow in responsibility through your guidance and through the delegation of responsibility to them. Your managers must feel free to act or you will find that all your time is being taken up with petty day-to-day decisions and you will not have the time left to handle the major things with which you must be concerned. An incentive program might be the answer at this time. Perhaps you will want to institute a bonus or other tangible reward for good work. Remember that people like to be recognized and rewarded and often the recognition is more important then the reward itself. Perhaps you could have an employee of the month featuring a picture on a poster in both shops. Maybe the reward could be a small plaque. How about a Sunday brunch for two at a nice restaurant? Something as simple as a

"Number One" button or pin can prove quite an inducement—anything the employee can show as a symbol of success. This type of incentive program works well for many major companies around the world. For ideas about incentives, contact your nearest Tupperware dealer or one of the other home-sales companies and ask what their company is doing for its employees. You probably won't be in a financial position to match a major company, but you should be able to get some good ideas.

As General Manager, you will want to spend some time making sure that all of your shops operate at the same level of excellence you expected of yourself when you opened your shop initially. If you keep service the key factor in your business, you can expect that business to thrive. As General Manager, you will wish to see that standards of cleanliness are maintained and that every employee lives up to your ideas about good customer relations. You would be well advised to see that there is a written policy with regard to the things you consider most important. In this way, no employee can accuse you (or one of your managers) of neglecting to inform him of the company policy. Many conflicts can be avoided in this way.

Ideally, as your business grows, you should find that you have more time to improve your own management skills. Who knows, perhaps you will eventually own a nationwide franchise of dog-grooming shops. Even the largest businesses in the world started with someone's dream.

15

We Also Offer . . .

Branching Out

THE SIMPLE FACT that you are in a business that offers a particular kind of care for pets will make you the first place your clients will look when they want other pet services and supplies. Whether or not you choose to branch out into some of the other pet-related services or the supply business will depend on several factors.

If you choose to branch out from your specialty, which is grooming, be sure that you really want to do so. If you don't like working with a retail business with all its attendant problems, if you aren't the least bit interested in dog training, if you just don't want your days off to be intruded upon by boarding animals, then perhaps you will elect to stick strictly to the grooming business and serve your customers by giving referrals to other businesses that can fill the other needs.

If you choose to remain a specialist, it will be very helpful to your clients if you are knowledgeable with regard to some of the other needs about which you are sure to be asked. Keeping in mind the fact that to your customer you are the ultimate authority on dogs, it will be in your own best interests to be sure that the places of business you recommend are reputable and honest. It will reflect badly upon you and your business if a client is treated poorly by a business to which you have sent him. Better to make no recommendation at all than to send your clients to a business that might give less than top-notch service or products.

SUPPLIES

The pet supply industry is a multimillion dollar business in the United States. If you decide that your grooming shop could benefit by having a share of the profits from this lucrative field, then you will be well advised to do your homework. Pet supplies run the gamut from items of real necessity, such as food, to the positively frivolous, such as fur coats and genuine diamond necklaces. It is most unlikely that you will try to stock every single item for dogs in your shop. You will need to make a careful assessment of your clientele and judge from their requests what items would be most profitable for you to stock.

Keeping in mind the fact that you will have a substantial amount of money tied up in your retail stock, you will want to choose items that will sell quickly and give you a good return on your investment. Exactly which items will work best for you will depend on your clientele and, to some extent, on your location. Unless you have a very elite business, it is unlikely that you will have a great demand for some of the luxury items, but you may have a real market for some of the fancy-looking but inexpensive collars and leashes that are available. If you live in a very warm climate few people will be interested in doggy sweaters, but you may do a booming business in wicker dog beds.

When planning your initial purchase of stock, you might want to conduct a survey of your customers to get an idea of the items they would like to find available in your shop. You could use a simple questionnaire to determine the items they have purchased within the past six months and items they would most like to have available. Grooming equipment, such as good quality brushes and combs, and supplies such as shampoo and flea powder are generally good sellers.

You may want to begin with only a few items and increase the amount of space devoted to retail sales as you see the need increasing. The very fact that you carry some items will lead your customers to request other things they would like to purchase. One way that you might get your retail sales off the ground is to contact any training clubs in the area and ask what equipment they require for students in their classes. If you are able to supply the items the trainers wish their students to use, you can usually expect to get some referrals from the obedience classes. As a bonus, these referrals will also make your business visible to folks who had not been aware of it before and who might be looking for a grooming shop.

Another way to plan for your retail sales is to make a careful survey to see what is available in other stores in your area. If you find that an item is not available and some of your clients have indicated an interest in that particular product, then it would probably be a good one for your salon to have in stock. If you have clients who want this product, then there are likely to be other people in the area who would also like to be able to purchase the same things.

No matter how much stock you carry, you are sure to find that you will have customers who want a particular item in a size or a color you do not have. If this is the case, you may wish to make arrangements to special-order for your customers. If you do this, it is wise to expect the customer to make a deposit (at least half the price is not unreasonable) on the special order. The "if we don't have it, we'll be glad to get it for you" attitude will make a nice impression on your clientele and will also allow you to please the customer as well as make a profit without having an enormous amount of your working capital invested in stock.

When you are considering retail sales, contact as many manufacturers as possible and find out what their wholesale policy is. Some will sell direct to you as an independent retailer, others will sell only to a middleman. Ask each manufacturer for a catalog with a wholesale-price list. It is amazing how much prices for comparable merchandise can vary. Some companies will even send merchandise to you on consignment, which essentially means that you pay for the amount of merchandise sold and send the rest back to the company. Be sure to ask about this kind of arrangement and be sure that you fully understand the terms. Failing to understand the exact terms of a consignment could result in having to pay for a large shipment of stock. Some companies will also send you samples of their merchandise so that you can inspect the quality of the items they are offering. Other companies have sales representatives who travel with sample merchandise so that you can look before you buy. In any case, if you are unsure about a product, be very sure that the company will back it with a money-back guarantee. This is not unreasonable and the better companies do offer this to their customers.

As with every other factor in your business, you will be the final word on quality control. It will be important to your business reputation that the retail items you choose to carry in your shop are items of good quality. You can only do yourself a disservice by carrying shabby merchandise. If you find that your customers are not happy with a particular item it will be in your own best interests to make whatever adjustment is necessary to achieve customer satisfaction. If the manufacturer with whom you are dealing is in fact selling top-quality items, you will usually find it will stand behind its products and will make an adjustment on defective merchandise.

Your aim is to keep your customer happy, and this can sometimes seem like an impossible task. You will need to be well enough informed about the various products you are carrying to be able to make a sound recommendation to your customers. If you are not able to answer the questions they will ask, you are likely to either lose the sale or to end up with a customer who is unhappy because the product was not the product he needed for the purpose he had in mind.

Retail sales can be an important part of your grooming-shop income if you research your market thoroughly and stock your shelves wisely. The initial work involved may seem like a lot, but if you do your homework well, retail sales can make a substantial contribution to your total income. The added advantage in having a section of your shop devoted to retail items is that you will have this as an added reason for people to stop in and get acquainted with your shop. Many of these people will subsequently become customers for the grooming business as well as for retail items.

What Shall I Stock at First?

Probably the best products for you to stock at the beginning of your venture into retailing as part of your grooming business will be some of those products that are closely related to the work you do.

One of the items you are almost sure to be asked about in a grooming shop is shampoo for use between visits. A good line of shampoo, creme rinse and perhaps cologne or powder to freshen up the pet will probably be one of your very best sellers. Whether you choose to sell the products you use in your own shop or to carry something packaged with the pet owner in mind is your own decision. It would be wise to at least try the various products so that you may make an informed recommendation. Perhaps you will want to carry several varieties of shampoo for different coat types or colors, or you may wish to feature one "exclusive" product. If the latter is your plan, you may want to prepare a poster exclaiming "We

Pegboard will hold a variety of treats and toys for sale.

use and recommend product X exclusively!" This poster could be displayed prominently in your waiting area.

Another line of products that is generally much in demand for the grooming salon is the flea-and-tick-control line. As you well know, there are many different products on the market. A good plan is to carry only those brands you know to be effective, and to carry each brand in several forms if possible. You might want to carry dip, powder and a spray all in the same brand if all three forms are made by the manufacturer. Whether or not you wish to carry the other items necessary for adequate parasite control is another matter. When you branch out into the products necessary for yard and household treatment, you may find that there are simply more items than you have either the space or the inclination to deal with. Also, when considering carrying pesticides of any kind, be sure that you are in compliance with your state and county requirements for the sale of these items. The laws vary substantially from one place to another, so some research could help you to avoid serious legal complications. If you are having a problem finding out the requirements for the sale of pesticides, check with a local exterminator to find out what agency issues exterminating licenses. That agency should be able to give you the information you will need to have so that you can make an informed decision with regard to the sale of pesticides.

BOARDING

Another very popular and lucrative addition to the services you offer is boarding care for your clients' pets. While boarding can add substantially to your overall income, it can also add substantially to your overhead as well. Boarding is a service that is frequently requested by the grooming-shop client and more than one shop owner has "backed" into the boarding business by caring for the occasional client's dog for the weekend or while that client was on vacation.

It is easy to be misled into thinking that boarding is easy money. Certainly caring for that one special customer's dog for just a few days doesn't seem like much work and the money paid for the service almost seems to be a windfall. One dog to care for isn't much trouble. Running a boarding kennel can be.

When considering the boarding business as an adjunct to your grooming salon, you will have to give much thought to the facility you now have and to what would be required to set up an adequate arrangement for boarding purposes. In making this decision, plan in advance whether you intend to limit yourself to small dogs only or if you will also accept large dogs for boarding. Remember that if you choose to board large dogs, you will have to have enough space for them to get their needed exercise and be comfortable. If you elect to board only small dogs, perhaps "cage" boarding will be adequate. If you will be doing cage boarding, you will still need to provide some space for the dogs to get exercise as well as for them to relieve themselves.

One of the most important points for you to consider when thinking of adding boarding to your business is that when you have animals in your care, someone must be available to care for those animals and to see that they remain clean, in good condition, well fed and comfortable. The most popular seasons for boarding are the very times when you might wish to take a day or two off yourself: Christmas Day, Thanksgiving Day, Easter, the Fourth of July. In fact, any major holiday is a day of business for a boarding facility. While your grooming shop will certainly see a rise in business during the days just prior to a holiday, the boarding business will be at its busiest on the holiday itself.

You will have to think about whether the demand for boarding will justify the necessary additions to your present facility, whether you will be able to afford to hire extra help to handle the boarding facility on the days that are not regular business days for your grooming shop and whether you are willing to be available should some emergency occur. You must be well aware that no employee is going to take your business as seriously as you do and few employees are going to be pleased to work on a major holiday. It is all too easy to find that an employee you had counted on to take care of all the boarders on a holiday has suddenly become "ill" and is unable to come to work. This leaves you with the ultimate responsibility for the care of those animals that are boarding with you during the holiday.

In considering adding boarding to your other services, read several of the good books on the subject that are available. The American Boarding Kennel Association has published a book about the boarding kennel business, and there are several others on the market. These books go into detail about the necessary facilities for boarding together with many other considerations. You would do

227

well to do some serious investigation on this particular subject. Boarding is a very necessary service for pets, but it can entail a great deal of time and effort as well as require extensive facilities. Visit as many boarding kennels as possible so that you can see for yourself just what is involved when you offer this as a regular service. Ask the kennel owner about the amount of time involved and about the availability of reliable kennel help.

Should you decide that you do not wish to add boarding to the list of services you can offer to your clients, your visits to area kennels should prepare you to refer your clients knowledgeably. The clients will appreciate the fact that you have actually paid a visit to the kennel in question and that you know what the facilities are like. You will also be in a position to send each client to a facility that is right for his pet. If your client owns a Great Dane, you will want to refer him to a kennel that has large runs available, and if he has a pampered Chihuahua, you may recommend a different kennel entirely. As with any referral you make, you will naturally try to refer only to those kennels in which you would consider leaving your own pet, and where you feel your client will receive good service for the fees he pays.

TRAINING

Here is still another area that could prove a lucrative addition to your grooming shop services if you are an experienced obedience trainer or have someone on your staff who is a trainer. You will find that many of your clients will ask about obedience training and some will ask about other kinds of training as well. Housebreaking, guard-dog training or even training for the show ring are popular. If you or someone who works for you is an obedience instructor, and if you have an adequate area available to you for a training class, and if you are willing to spend the necessary time to conduct a class, this can be a nice little supplement to your income.

Obedience classes can return a nice profit for the amount of time invested, presuming that you have the space for the class. Most classes meet for about one hour once each week. The owners are then instructed to practice with their dogs daily. The average class might be ten to fifteen students and might last ten weeks. You can see that this is essentially ten hours of your time spent in teaching the class.

If you are an experienced obedience instructor, you can use

your grooming shop to publicize the training classes you will be offering. You will find that many of your clients will be glad to find that a class is available to them and will enroll and perhaps bring friends as well. The class can help build your grooming-shop clientele also because people will attend the class who are not already patrons of your place of business.

Teaching an obedience-training class is not a position for the inexperienced. This is a position that requires knowledge and ability. If you are not an instructor and you do not have an instructor on your staff, you will do well to reconsider the idea of offering obedience classes. If you are genuinely interested in the art of dog training, contact the nearest obedience-training club and inquire about their instructor-training program. In general, you will find that an instructor-training program will be involved and time-consuming.

If you are not an instructor, do not have an instructor on your payroll and do not want to spend the time to learn how to be an obedience trainer, then, like the boarding kennel situation, be ready to make a recommendation to your clients. If there are several obedience classes available in your area, contact the organizations that conduct these classes and ask if they will be sure to keep you posted about the dates and times their classes begin. If you want to do a thorough job and be able to make a sound recommendation to your customers, you may wish to visit each of the training classes, see how the class is conducted and perhaps talk with some of the people who have taken the class previously. If you are not particularly interested in attending various classes or if you feel unqualified to make a judgment about the value of the different classes, then be ready to say as much when your customers ask about training. You will be far better off in the long run if you simply suggest that your clients check out the classes for themselves. In this way, you are disassociating yourself and your place of business from the classes and it is to be hoped your clients will understand that you are not making a recommendation as such. This is especially important for you to consider with regard to training classes because students in a dog-training class may tend to become quite emotional about their success or failure in the class and will virtually never accept the responsibility for whether or not their dogs do well in the class, tending rather to blame the instructor for poor training, and ultimately blaming you for having recommended the class.

Branching out can be a real asset to your business or it can be nothing more than a time-consuming problem. This is something that only you can decide. Many businesses successfully combine grooming with boarding, training and retail sales, others specialize in one facet and do just as well as the businesses that offer several different services. Your choice is your own. As long as you investigate, study and plan your expansion, you will be able to decide for yourself whether or not you wish to specialize or go for a wider variety of services.

16

Listen, That Other Shop . . .

Professional Relationships

UNLESS YOU ARE in the unusual position of being totally isolated in the geographic area in which you will be working, it is inevitable that you will have at least some contact with other groomers in your vicinity. That contact can be a pleasant professional relationship or it can be a petty, back-stabbing feud. Although you will not, of course, be in control with regard to the behavior and attitudes of other dog groomers in your area, you can certainly control your own attitudes, and you can resolve to behave as the professional person that you are regardless of the behavior of others.

GETTING ACQUAINTED

The first step toward forming a professional relationship, like any other relationship, is to get acquainted. Perhaps you are already on at least a speaking basis with one or two of the other groomers in the city where you have decided to open your shop (or in the area into which you are moving as you branch out, if this is a second or third salon for you) and can simply make the announcement that you will be opening a grooming shop and hope that you will have a long and pleasant business friendship. If there is a groomers' association in your vicinity, you may wish to join or at least to visit and see if it is the sort of organization you would like to join. If there is such an organization, it will at the very least serve the purpose of helping you to meet many of the people who are in the same business you are in and who share some of the same interests and goals that you have.

If you don't know anyone at all in the business, you may find that getting to know people can be a bit more difficult. One way to get to know other groomers is to drop in at their place of business, introduce yourself and perhaps invite them to an open house at your new salon. Do not be surprised if the reception you receive is somewhat chilly. There does seem to be an unfortunate tendency for groomers to be a bit standoffish and inclined to resent a new shop owner in what they consider to be their territory. It is assumed that you have done your research well and that the area in which you will be opening your grooming shop is not saturated with other groomers. If this is the case, then you are not going to be any actual threat to anyone with regard to taking away their business. By the same token, when other new groomers open salons in your vicinity, you will not need to worry that they will hurt your business. Competition in business is a normal, healthy situation.

When you are in the getting-acquainted stage, you may be surprised to hear some groomers make extremely negative remarks about other groomers' work or their ethics or their facilities. Again, this is simply a form of pettiness that is all too common, and it is to be hoped that you will not take any of these remarks seriously and that you certainly will not pass them on.

Forming a Groomers' Association

If there is no groomers' organization within a reasonable distance of your location, you might want to organize one. The primary purpose of such an organization would be to share information and to foster better professional relationships between groomers within the association. If you already know one or two other groomers, enlist their aid in bringing people together for the purpose of discussing the development of this kind of group. If a groomers' association is well thought out and well planned, it can be of great benefit to its members, to the members' clientele and to the community. In some large cities, the dog-groomers' association spends one evening each month doing grooming for the local humane shelter. This, of course, results in more stray animals being placed in good homes and, in a roundabout way, tends to build the grooming business both through the increased number of pets and through the favorable publicity that is generated from this charitable work. It might be added that the groomers who take part also enjoy the sociability and feel great satisfaction in knowing they have done a real service.

It would be to the advantage of dog groomers within a groomers' organization to have as a guest speaker a veterinarian who might discuss the best methods for control of external parasites. Another topic might be emergency first aid with special emphasis on problems that might occur in a grooming-shop situation. As a rule, veterinarians are readily available for such lectures, and if a question-and-answer session follows the presentation, even more benefit can be reaped. Another problem faced in every grooming shop is that of taxes. Perhaps it would be possible to arrange for a guest speaker on the subject of taxes. This could be someone who specializes in income tax preparation, a lawyer who specializes in taxes or perhaps someone who teaches courses in income tax preparation at a nearby college or university.

The members themselves could present programs illustrating their own techniques for various types of grooming, or perhaps someone could show how a particular problem is handled in his salon. These are just a few ideas that could be used within a groomers' association. If such an organization is to function and grow, it must provide a service for its members as well as the opportunity to share a social time together. Ideally, a professional association of this nature will foster good business relationships, will provide a forum for the members to discuss various business situations that arise and will in general help its members to grow and develop.

Related Fields

When getting acquainted with the other groomers in your area, you might also wish to make the acquaintance of the other professionals in related fields. This includes veterinarians, kennel owners or managers, and obedience instructors. All of these people will be involved with clients of yours from time to time and the more people you know in these related businesses, the better prepared you will be in many ways. It can be of great help to your customers if you are able to make an informed recommendation with regard to a kennel facility or a veterinarian or an obedience class, and the better acquainted you are with the people who are offering these services, the better prepared you will be to make this kind of recommendation.

Not only will your customers benefit from your becoming acquainted with other professionals, but you and your business will profit also. You are much more likely to get referrals from people in these related businesses if they have met you and have been favorably impressed with your professional attitude.

Your desire for referrals is also a good reason to give thought to holding a reception in your new grooming shop and making it an invitation-only affair limited to all those people in your particular location who are involved in any of the dog-related businesses. This will give you an opportunity to meet these various individuals, and it will give them a chance to see your facility and to be aware of the care and planning you have put into your establishment. If you later choose to hold an open house for the general public, that should be an entirely different kind of get-together.

GOSSIP AND COMPLAINTS

When you first open your doors, you may have some clients who will tell you all manner of horror stories about other shops to which they have taken their pets. It is possible that some of the stories you hear will be nothing but the unvarnished truth, but it is also possible that what you are told will be only a carefully-edited version of the truth. Some of the people who come to you with a sad tale of how their pet was mistreated at a certain shop will neglect to tell you that the pet was a little terror and bit the groomer three times before he was finally finished.

Naturally, you will listen to the things told to you by your customers. It is a good idea to listen, make a mental note and simply file the information for future thought. In listening to your customers tell tales about the various groomers in town, listen between the lines, so to speak. Often just by listening to the client's story, you will be able to avoid making the same mistake that aroused his anger previously. If the client says, "They cut Fifi's toenails so short that they bled," you will know right away that this customer does not want those nails to be cut extremely short. The same will apply to criticism of the style in which the dog was clipped. Careful listening can help you avoid many pitfalls.

Just as you will hear criticism of other groomers, you will also hear negative comments made about area veterinarians and kennels. These will cover a wide range of complaints, some valid and some altogether frivolous. Even though the criticisms are made about another facet of dog care, listen carefully. The client is giving you a great deal of information about himself and about his likes and dislikes. If you keep this information in mind, you will be able to please the customer better and will be more likely to keep his business. Even though you feel sure that the customer's complaint is not based on fact, one thing remains true and that is that the client is not satisfied with the service he received, and as a result may take his business to another veterinarian or kennel in the future.

When listening to the various complaints you will hear, keep in mind that you can't please all of the people all of the time. You (and every other groomer, veterinarian and kennel owner) can only do your very best, and even that will fall short in some cases. Some people simply cannot be pleased no matter how hard you try. Others may be impossible for one groomer to deal with yet be the absolute delight of another groomer. Much of this can be attributed to a matter of personalities. If you are tempted to believe what your customers tell you about various other salons, keep in mind that some of the same stories will be told about you as time goes on. In the interest of good business relations with the customer, you will do well to listen and say little one way or the other. If the client asks you directly whether a certain procedure is correct, a tactful way to answer is to simply say, "In our shop, we do thus and so, but there are many ways to accomplish most things." This doesn't reflect badly on the other groomer, yet it doesn't put you in the position of challenging the client either. Another way to handle this sort of questioning is to nod and say, "I can tell that you weren't very pleased with that." Again, you have simply understood what your client was saying without criticizing another professional person. This may not seem important to you right now, but as you continue in this business, you will develop a real understanding of the importance of maintaining a professional attitude and of withholding your comments about the work done by others.

Silence is Golden

One of the most important lessons you can learn is to maintain professional silence. You will avoid more problems with silence than with most other professional attributes. Sometime it takes a real effort not to make that disparaging remark, but the effort is not a futile one. Critical remarks have an unfortunate way of coming back to haunt the maker.

Gossip is a great temptation to most people, but gossip can be ruinous to a business. What customer wants to patronize a place of business that he feels is likely to gossip about the way he cares for his pet or the special services he expects? Your customer must be able to confide in you. He must be able to tell you that he is concerned about fleas without being afraid that you will be critical of him, perhaps telling someone else that he doesn't take good care of his dog. This is a matter of real concern to your clients. Many people feel that you are criticizing their housekeeping if you explain that fleas can and do infest carpets and furniture. These folks certainly don't want you to tell other people that they have a problem with these pests. Even if you think that a client is ridiculous, you must be very careful not to say so. Even though you do not use names, sometimes a story is so thinly disguised that the individual is well aware that he is the butt of your joke, and you can be sure that he will not like being in that position. Even though the story you tell might have nothing to do with the client who hears it, he will always wonder if you might later tell something about him. In addition, the person to whom you tell a story could be the very best friend of the person about whom you are speaking. You could lose the business of both parties and never know why you had lost these two clients.

Silence with regard to other businesses is also the mark of a professional individual. It reflects well upon you and upon your business practices if you maintain a discreet silence about the business practices of others. Not only does this discretion reflect well on you, but it will enhance your standing with other professional people when they know that you do not indulge in gossip or pettiness. This policy is especially true with regard to other grooming businesses and other groomers. These people are your competitors, but they are also your business associates. Neither they nor your clients will have much respect for you if you must make derogatory remarks about others in your own profession in order to impress people with the quality of your work. Remember that real quality stands upon its own merits and need not criticize the merits of others in order to be appreciated.

When thinking of maintaining a discreet silence with regard to other businesses, you will have to be concerned with other grooming shops, but you should grant the same courtesy to other related fields as well. Kennels will be among those you will hear criticized by your customers, as will trainers and, especially, veterinarians. All of these related fields will, in a sense, be involved in your general area of interest and expertise. Some of the stories you will hear will be hair-raising and you may be tempted to accept these stories as truth. Perhaps they are truth. And perhaps they are not. The real danger here is that you may be led to make a judgment without a sufficient fund of information. Try to avoid making this sort of judgment, or at least avoid passing it along to your customers. Not only is it a poor business practice, but you might even find yourself involved in a lawsuit.

You Are Entitled to Your Own Opinions

All of these cautions with regard to professional silence are not meant to indicate that you should not have your own opinions. Of course you will have your own opinions, and in some cases, you will feel that you simply are not in agreement with the business practices of some other business and for that reason do not wish to refer anyone to that shop, kennel or office. If you are asked for a referral to a kennel, for instance, you are certainly going to prefer to recommend a kennel you feel will be able to serve your clients' needs. Not only will you wish to do this to be of assistance to your clients, but also because you know that, in a roundabout way, your referrals do reflect upon you.

What if you are asked directly about a business you do not recommend? One good way to handle this is to say something like, "We normally send people to Brand-X Kennel and if they are full, we suggest you call Z's Kennel." If the inquirer persists, you can feel free to say, "We don't usually send people to the kennel you are asking about, but if you are interested in it, why don't you go there for a visit?" Once in a while you will be faced with someone who is insistent upon knowing why you don't send people to that particular kennel and you may have to be quite firm with your statement that, "We do not make it a practice to make any judgmental remarks about another place of business. When making referrals, we try to send people to places we feel sure will give them the kind of good service we like to give our clients here." If said pleasantly and firmly, this will usually get you off the hook without having to make any sort of derogatory remark. You can use the same basic format with regard to veterinarians, obedience schools and pet shops.

If you are seriously involved in dog breeding and feel that pet shops are not a good place to purchase puppies, you have the right to that opinion and, if asked, can choose a tactful way to say as much. If you do say this however, try to be prepared to offer the questioner an alternative way to find a pup of the breed in which he is interested.

In the final analysis, the more professional you are in your attitudes and behavior, the better liked you will be in the business community, and in the long run this is all to your benefit. Even though you may not agree with the business practices you see around you, your professional silence will earn respect for you from both clients and associates. Petty behavior, on the other hand, makes you look little better than the business you are criticizing.

Afterword

W HEN ALL IS said and done, the real deciding factor in your success or failure as a dog groomer (from the profit-making point of view) lies in your own hands and in your own attitudes. People have begun businesses of all kinds and made a real success even though they began with little or nothing in the way of financial backing. Other people have started businesses with plenty of capital and have failed miserably. Your own determination, hard work and dedication to making a success of this business will see you through. It is important that you set your goals and work toward them—don't be afraid to set them high. If you dream of a chain of grooming shops, then go for it. Every journey begins with the first step and the first step is to decide what you want. Next, look to see how you can make the first move in that direction. Perhaps it will be to work for someone else for a time, but don't let that keep you from your dreams and plans. Never lose sight of your goal.

Remember that the information in this book is a guide, not a set of hard-and-fast rules. The suggestions here are made from experience, but that doesn't mean that your own ideas won't work. Never be afraid to try. Grooming businesses are very individual and that individuality is the key to their success. Because people are so involved with their pets, they have certain ideas about how their particular pets should be cared for, and one grooming salon is not likely to please every single pet owner. Your very personality may be just exactly what a large group of people want when they look for a grooming shop. Let who you are shine through. Your honesty, sincerity and caring can make this new venture a rousing success, and while it is becoming a success it can make you a nice income as well. Look around you at the major companies that began with a dream (and often little more than that) and are now thriving, nationally known businesses. Each of them, just like you, has found a need, and by filling that need has found success.